MOTHER ISLAND

MOTHER ISLAND

A DAUGHTER CLAIMS PUERTO RICO

Jamie Figueroa

PANTHEON BOOKS

NEW YORK

Copyright © 2024 by Jamie Figueroa

Grateful acknowledgment is made to Beacon Press for permission to reprint an excerpt of "Revision" by Aurora Levine Morales from *Women Writing Resistance* by Jennifer Browdy. Reprinted by permission of Beacon Press, Boston.

LIBRARY OF CONGRESS CATALOGING-IN-PUBLICATION DATA
Name: Figueroa, Jamie, author.
Title: Mother island / Jamie Figueroa.
Description: First edition. New York : Pantheon Books, 2024
Identifiers: LCCN 2023029793 (print). LCCN 2023029794 (ebook). ISBN 9780553387681 (hardcover). ISBN 9780553387698 (ebook)
Subjects: LCSH: Figueroa, Jamie. | Puerto Rican women—Ohio—Biography. | Puerto Rican women—Ohio—Ethnic identity. | Mothers and daughters—Ohio. | Puerto Rican women—New Mexico—Santa Fe Biography. | Puerto Rican women—New Mexico—Santa Fe—Ethnic identity. | Figueroa, Jamie—Travel—Puerto Rico—San Juan. | San Juan (P.R.) —Social life and customs. | Santa Fe (N.M.)—Biography. | Ohio—Biography.
Classification: LCC F496.4.F54 A3 2024 (print) | LCC F496.4.F54 (ebook) | DDC 305.868/7295092 [B]—dc23/eng/20230712
LC record available at https://lccn.loc.gov/2023029793
LC ebook record available at https://lccn.loc.gov/2023029794

www.pantheonbooks.com

Jacket illustration based on original art by Luciano Cian (image details added from alexhstock / Getty Images, joakimbkk / Getty Images, ivanastar / Getty Images, and LuminatePhotos by Judith / Shutterstock)
Jacket design by Emily Mahon

Printed in the United States of America

FIRST EDITION

2 4 6 8 9 7 5 3 1

"One role of the artist is to document the now for the yet to come."

—MOIRA PERNAMBUCO, FROM THE EXHIBITION
ANCESTORS KNOW WHO WE ARE

For those who have come before
and for those yet to come

CONTENTS

*"We must prevail over the times we are living in
with the help of our ancestors."*

—RIGOBERTA MENCHÚ

*"... They began to fulfil the destiny which was concealed
in the marrow of their bones ..."*

—*POPOL VUH*

AUTHOR'S NOTE

In 2011, while finally completing my BFA in Creative Writing after a fifteen-year break from being a full-time student, I put together an experimental manuscript of creative nonfiction entitled *The Hem of Skin*. Part poetry, part stage play, part scene vignettes, and part epistolary, the manuscript fiercely confronted secrets and rumors, interrogating the generational trauma of being removed from, discarded by, and distanced from extended family and from la tierra madre, Puerto Rico/Borikén, while constellating my experiences as a descendant of those who survived over five hundred years of ongoing colonization.

It dug at the soul wounds inflicted by colonization and imperialism, the masks of assimilation, and the contortions of adaptation. It dug at the mother-daughter root, the sister root, and my own identity root, as I had first fashioned a sense of self woven from my mother's and older sisters' hand-me-downs of womanhood. My intention had been to show what was under the shame and the shoulds of oppression. A people who had survived—creative, powerful, sovereign.

What became of that manuscript was every budding memoirist's nightmare. After it placed in a small press contest and the first essay, "Is It True?," was made public (which I proudly shared on my Facebook page at the time), my mother's sister—who is also my godmother—was incensed. As was her right. Not only was I asking a series of questions that threatened all that she and her siblings had endured to embed themselves in the dominant culture, all that they had survived, but I also used their names. She wrote a letter to the editor demanding it be removed from the press's website, citing the metaphors and poetic language as evidence of falsehoods, not functions of crafted language, style, and voice. She stated that I was a liar, a storyteller, not to be trusted, and in that letter, she disowned me on behalf of all her siblings—my aunts and uncles.

I should not have used their real names.

Shortly after, my phone in New Mexico rang my aunt's in Minnesota. She would not pick up, so I left a message on her answering machine. *I'm sorry to have caused you such distress.* Instead of discussing her experience with me, she preferred to process it with my mother, who, in turn, never warned me about any of it, never shared a single word about the upset brewing, the damning letter disowning me and calling my newly emerging career as a writer, my lifelong dream, into question.

Tía, lo siento.

Not for telling my story my own way, which is my inherent birthright, but for the pain and hurt that I unintentionally caused. Since that time of manuscript trauma and recovery, I have continued to navigate generational rupture. It is a consistent and invasive presence. I've come to personally understand Audre Lorde's warning, "Your silence will not protect you."

My silence will not/has not protect/ed me. I will not avert my eyes.

May these pages be an affirmation of and an invitation for all the many iterations of story and identity, of ancestry and belonging, of place and survivance, there are. We are desperate for them all.

MOTHER ISLAND

"Water never goes away; it only keeps returning in new form. That is the science, and that is the story."

—TIPHANIE YANIQUE, *MONSTER IN THE MIDDLE*

THE STORIES I HAVEN'T
BEEN TOLD

IN MY LATE TWENTIES, DURING MY SATURN RETURN—WHEN, according to astrology, the transition into adulthood is fully realized—I moved to Santa Fe, New Mexico, a place I'd been regularly visiting for nearly eight years. I rented a room in the home of an elderly woman, a divorcée from Texas. Her eastside condo faced north. Floor-to-ceiling windows showcased Mount Baldy at an intimate distance, relaxed in its pose. I beheld it every day and imagined it beholding me as well. It was a kind of worship, meditation, communion.

I found work at an internationally renowned spa where a hierarchy of massage therapists crowded the schedule months in advance, leaving hours available only by subbing shifts. As I waited for bookings, I slow-walked; I stood; I stared at the mountain, the hills, the sky, and the vast distances where other mountains and mesas seemed temporarily paused in their own great ongoing transformation. I used this as tangible evidence of beauty, of stability, of possibility.

There was no money for such a relocation. I'd borrowed what I could. My credit cards were maxed out after a recent divorce, and I had no savings, so I stayed to the trails, to the generosity, acceptance, and inclusion of Mother Earth/Mother Nature.

Mountains, mesas, piñons, ponderosa pines, pine, juniper, cedar, chamisa, cholla, prickly pear, sage. Whispers of water called river. The way that water whispers. Female rain. Coyotes, bears, snakes, wild cats, wild horses. Sky. All of this and more rearranged my reality. It was an external and an internal experience. Because of this, I could soften and strengthen simultaneously. A teaching from the mountain, as if it were an eternal mother.

These shared, free, public lands evoked a similar sensation to the one I cultivated in my notebook. I was disoriented and overcome with vulnerability. Everything I did and said seemed awkward to me. I was unfamiliar to myself in this new home.

I held to my pen, translated my details into language.

Maps of Puerto Rico, Ohio, and New Mexico were taped to my bedroom wall. After printing them, I traced each border with my fingers, tried to understand how these shapes had shaped me. My triptych of un/belonging. Puerto Rico, the Island of Enchantment. New Mexico, the Land of Enchantment. And there in between, Ohio, where I had grown up—its state border resembling a crude heart, a bridge that I spent my younger years crossing.

If only I could get my coordinates right. I wished locating myself were as easy as looking at these maps.

As I shed my experience as a tourist and transformed into a resident, I considered how to introduce myself—what stories I wanted to share and how I would present them. Most other transplants assumed I was Nuyorican. (I did not confess that I'd been to New York City only once, for a few hours as a child, while visiting my tío's family in a New Jersey suburb. The lively alleyways, yellow taxicabs, mounds of trash, and buildings rising endlessly above me as if into and beyond the sky were my singular tangible and daunting memory.) Santa Fe locals spoke to me first in Spanish.

New Mexico was not Ohio, obviously and thankfully. Neck tattoos of BROWN POWER were not uncommon, most public places were bilingual, checkout ladies at the grocery store and in government offices called me "mi'ja," the closest I'd ever come to my mother's "mi'jita." No one asked me what I was. Occasionally, I was asked where I or my people were from, not as an interrogation, or to single out and exclude, but as an invitation, to welcome and include.

The white body supremacy of the Midwest, polite but persistent racism, and the confines of small-town culture dissolved. There was more room to explore my own identity. To coax out what I had banished to the corners for fear of being unsafe. This is how it was for me, a mixed-race woman of color, who had tried to mimic whiteness as my mother had. I constantly had to wave my white flag of surrender at what and who oppressed me, as if to say, *Please, have mercy. I will not be a threat to you.*

Liberated from Ohio, and the conditioning of my submissive youth, I set out to try to understand and claim what colonization had stolen from my family, from me, what it continued to steal. If I was not hiding, who was I? If I was not adapting to what was acceptable to those who couldn't even truly see me to begin with, who could I become? When you pull out the weeds of colonization, how do you tend to what's always been there, growing, albeit concealed?

These were the questions that continued to remake and reshape me. After a fifteen-year break from academia, I finished my education at a tribal college, the Institute of American Indian Arts. That is where these questions were seeded, germinated, and took root. I also "returned" for the first time to my family's homeland, the island of Puerto Rico. Called Borikén by the original people, the Taíno, who are my ancestors.

———

In my memory, it was exactly like this:

My mother and my two older sisters lie on a nubbly yellow felt blanket in the grass. The top edge is lined in unraveling satin. Kneeling behind my mother, I study her and my teenage sisters. Their arms and legs are longer than anything I have yet to experience—potential and self-possession outstretched—and browning darker by the moment.

I hold a small lined notebook in my left hand. The pencil I use is dull; the soft, blunt lead digs into the spaces between the blue lines. On this first page, I am careful to make the stems of the *h*'s and *d*'s tall. Careful to hook the *g* in the right direction. I can write a handful of two- and three-letter words. The spiral on the side of the notebook glints, catching the sun as the wire coil shifts in response to the pressure of my writing. Creativity moves naturally from the center of my being down my right arm and through my hand with each carefully crafted letter. At six years old, I compose my first poem.

Uninterrupted by trees, the backyard is vast. It rolls into one neighbor's lawn and then another as far as can be seen. Tufts of dandelions in full bloom, and in post-blossom puff, constellate the grass. Prince plays from a small speaker lodged in one of the upstairs windows. We shriek and call out with our passionate imitations as he cries, "Purple rain." The back of the split-level seems to turn away from us, more interested in the road and who might be passing by than in our emotional outburst. Awaiting its master, our mother's new husband, as if some obedient pet. We have similarly adapted and learned to wait for commands in his presence.

It is early spring. The prior autumn, my mother, my sisters, and I had packed the contents of our government housing—a subsidized duplex—into large black trash bags and piled them into the family car, a two-door maroon Buick. We drove a few towns south from our neighborhood of Black and brown mothers and children adorned with beaded hair to move in with our mother's new husband, whose home had too many empty rooms, since his own children were adults. Before this, all four of us had slept in one bed each night. My earliest memory of sleeping and dreaming was of being lodged between the bodies of a pair of older sisters, only sixteen months apart, and our mother. After we moved, I didn't have the capacity to express the longing I felt for that bed, for the exclusive unit we were, a family of the feminine. A womb of our own containment and authority, safe. To be with this man in his house, each of us in our own room, my mother the farthest away she'd ever been, was a betrayal of what I had come to know and trust.

As daughters, we were no longer privileged. As the youngest, I was no longer preferred. There was a man now, a white man, with a white and silver tinseled beard and white T-shirts with tinted stains beneath his arms, and white cigarettes with endless plumes of white smoke snaking around him at the head of the table as he regaled us with endless stories from his shift at the Goodyear plant after every dinner.

He rearranged our hierarchy. My mother submitted. In my limited understanding, I was confused about how this had happened. I wanted it undone. But in the grass that day, on the blanket with my real family, each one of them stretched out, singing, laughing, radiating the comfort of the familiar, I was compelled to summon the sparse language that I possessed to capture what I belonged to and what belonged to me. Grass, flowers, trees, sun, laughter. Nearly all the words misspelled. A list more than a poem, as if art were an act of inventory, an exercise of naming. No matter. It was my moment: my mother, my sisters, my pencil, my paper. A celebration.

This was before we ran, never to return. Before the next man came along—one husband after another and all the boyfriends in between, traversing our lives, rearranging us as they came and went, scrambling the cohesion of our feminine collective.

———

How long did the pastor and his family take us in for when we left— was it a week, a month? I don't remember how many times we moved. Canal Fulton, Bellefontaine, Plain City, Marysville. Mount Vernon, Delaware, East Liberty. And then there were the counties: Union, Morrow, Knox, Logan, Licking, Hocking. Thirty miles in all directions radiating from the intersection of Main and Maple. The fields sliced by long lines of unused, nameless railroad tracks. On two-lane county roads, clapboard houses leaned from their foundations as if preparing to pick up, at long last, and begin their migration, as if they were never from here either. In between the houses and pole barns, men's briefs, socks, and undershirts—all white—and denim jeans of all sizes hung on clotheslines, stiff with the memory of their owner's thighs and knees in the winter air. In these lands, the only darkness came with the skin of night. Rural Ohio. We would cross another county line to another Main Street, where semitrucks had worn grooves in the asphalt; where the drive-through liquor store was not far from the collection of churches; and, of course, where there were more fields—feed corn, soybeans— and cows in various group formations, as if painted boulders, the most uninterested of us all.

I don't remember where I thought I was going when, at six years old, shortly before we ran, I put a pack of bubble gum, a photo of my mother, my nightgown, and two pairs of underwear into a brown paper sack and stomped out the front door. Perhaps I thought that I could find what I no longer had, that by leaving I could somehow go back to the place where I was still included in my own family—unquestioned belonging.

I did not manage to pull off my escape. My sisters ran after me, dragging me back to the house. Laughing and crying at my ridiculous choice of what to pack, at my courage and desperation. At our desperation. I would learn in the coming years to go missing in other ways.

I don't remember the look on my mother's face later that night when she returned from work, hours on her feet cutting hair, and they told her. Surely it was a terrible mix of hurt and other emotions too numerous to track, let alone name. The hurt that had been unleashed on her. The hurt she unleashed on me. The hurt I learned to return.

I don't remember how many years I used that same kind of brown paper sack as a book bag. I don't remember how many times I was asked, "What are you?" How many classroom windows I stared out of as if held hostage by a room full of people who did not look like me, aching for some semblance of the familiar, for something nourishing, to be claimed. The weapon of education was wielded, a highly edited history unquestioned, purposefully excluding me while demanding my subservience in return. Another kind of assault, of trauma, that of being invisible, of being silenced, of being rewarded/punished for loyalty or lack thereof to the sameness I was drowning in—soundlikelookliketalklike thinklikeactlike.

In recent years, we've learned more and more about trauma, memory, and the brain. A multitude of studies have been released detailing up-to-date science about the relationship between these and how each functions. One can read through a number of medical journals or psychology blogs and piece together a basic understanding. Trauma can be defined as anything that overwhelms the nervous system. Trauma affects memory and cognitive function. Trauma steals our ability to recall the basic details of our stories. In their place, blanks. Our ability to perceive and translate experience into story, which in turn helps us make meaning, is impaired by trauma.

Trauma affects our ability to imagine.

If you subscribe to the information revealed by epigenetics, you have within each of your cells approximately three generations of trauma—your body, the recordkeeper. An inheritance of emotional history. "Remembering," as Belarusian poet Valzhyna Mort explains in an interview about her latest book of poems, *Music for the Dead and Resurrected,* "not how it was, but how it felt."

My memory is affected by the trauma my ancestors experienced in their lives as well as by my own trauma. My mother's story is also *my* story, as are the stories of my grandparents, and my great-grandparents. The handful of explicit details I recall, often strange and incoherent—lost, found, lost—are assembled and reassembled.

And, of course, there are all the blanks.

I don't remember how many times I was assigned to fill out my family tree—blank after blank after blank. My mother shrugged her shoulders, defeat in her body as she looked at the stump of it. What kind of person can't name those from whom they are descended?

I remember the surprise of digging up potatoes for the first time the summer we were free from men again—a brief intermission—my nails thick with dark, moist Ohio soil. I remember my mother opening her first barbershop. I remember roaming the woods behind our newly constructed condo, each tree extending a welcome I rarely experienced from other humans, where I wished on mini-toads and lay against the ground, conjuring forest spirits, contemplating clouds, whispering to the winged ones—a place to belong as I once had among the bodies of my mother and my sisters. And then another suitor, another wedding, and the beginning of my mother's third marriage.

I was nine years old the first time I was asked what I was, what my "nationality" was. A group of neighborhood mothers surrounded me, their voices not altogether unkind but insistent.

Later, alone with my mother, her response—Puerto Rican.

Two unfamiliar words.

What exactly was an island?

Where exactly did this island exist?

What exactly was an ocean?

The confusion of it all.

Was it the year before that she had shown me *West Side Story* on VHS tape as she slept on the couch after a long day of standing on her feet? And that, soon after, my sister forced me to watch *Scarface* with her? As machine guns tore through one scene and then another, she gripped me tighter, enthralled by the violence. I kept my eyes closed, but the sound stayed in my head for days, weeks. Caribbean gangsters, criminals. I wasn't sure what either of these movies had to do with us.

What they couldn't explain and what would take me nearly forty years to articulate was that as a descendant of la isla living in the Midwest, separated from her language, culture, ancestry, and living history—her ecosystem—my mother did not know how to define herself on her own terms. She did not trust her own experience of herself.

As a lighter-skinned Boricua, a color closer to café con leche than café (clearly not white American but able to skirt the edges of her Black/brown, Afro-Taíno identity), she defined herself only by how others saw her: "exotic," mysterious, beautiful—and privileged their experience of her instead.

———

My family comes from an island that is owned by the United States of America. Property, not a state. After losing the Spanish-American War in 1898, Spain surrendered Puerto Rico to the U.S., which benefited economically and militarily as the island proved to be a key strategic location for bases while providing soldiers for wars, beginning with World War I. Infantry units were racially segregated until the 1950s. Citizenship, but not equal inclusion. "Like a loyal battered wife who will never leave her abusive husband," is how a Brazilian acquaintance once described the island in relation to the mainland. There is no vote on the island that counts across the official border. You have no voice in Congress or the White House when you are located between San Juan and Ponce, between Mayagüez and Luquillo. Only when you are a (Puerto Rican) resident of Florida, Minnesota, New York, Iowa do you have federal voting rights. Only when you are in the arms of the mainland, within the empire's grip. This access to U.S. soil is more than other islanders have throughout the Caribbean. A leash of privilege even if short in its reach.

The story that I assemble from scraps is that my mother's father, Aniceto, left the island in search of work sometime in the early 1940s. Before he departed, he took all ten of his children to live with his sister and brother-in-law in Rio Piedras—a suburb of San Juan—where they were cared for with the help of the money he sent as often as he could. One by one, following the infection of my eldest aunt's eye (and subsequent blindness), each of the ten children was sent to New York City. There is never any mention of his wife—my grandmother Aida—in the migration. But at some point, she is also in New York City. She appears and disappears. Once in the city, the eldest children were expected to fend for themselves. The youngest three were handled differently.

"I kept you. At least you had a mother."

I come from the sound of mangos thumping against the ground at night, let loose from the only branches they've known. I come from the songs of coquí. I come from cats that pour off roofs; huddle in dry, unused fountains; and clutter in shadows. I come from my grandfather's dark-skinned mother, who, sitting in her wheelchair, held each one of her grandchildren close to her heart like the gold they were. I come from the bed where my mother and all her siblings slept, with a hole in the middle that they had to navigate for fear of falling. I come from ebony cousins who became the monsters in my mother's warning stories of whom to fear—the darkness hidden inside you, yourself. I come from poverty, birds hunted by slingshot, winged food. I come from the stones in the river, the roots of the mangrove, the surprise of stars glittering in the water of the lagoon—wonders present generations before Columbus was born.

Assimilation feels not so much like being erased as being painted over—with thick layers of whitewash—until a blank surface has been created on which the dominant culture asserts itself, produces a replica of itself. And while for some newcomers to this country (those who are white with a European accent and access to wealth—their own or their family's) it may seem like a choice, for others it is implicit, expected. Survival. Prohibition, from the Latin *prohibitus,* "holding back." Prohibition of our languages and the free expression of cultures. And there's what is forced, a single understanding of God—constricting the Divine into an experience so narrow, so sharp, it manifests as violence against the body, violence against the mind, violence against the spirit, violence against the heart. Rules and behaviors consistent with those of the dominant culture, asserted by white body supremacy—must be navigated on a daily basis. Something BIPOC communities and LGBTQIA2S+ communities also know well.

What we need to understand is that neither trauma, memory, nor the brain is static or unchanging/unchangeable. Rather, they are living, breathing, and transforming. Feral. They leave their trace. Trauma has its own intelligence and force; it is alive in all those who have survived it. It's alive in the descendants of those who were afflicted by it. First, second, and third generations (I would argue more) have the scars, the same pattern of teeth marks and claw marks, found in the generation who suffered the direct harm. Memory will shape-shift with age and time and perspective. Its fins become wings; wings become hide, legs, tail. Horns emerge. It seems to control you, not the other way around. And the brain? Some ninety percent, undecipherable. All that gray matter. A whole universe inside our skulls that even the most well-versed in the field will confess is unknown.

Assimilation, even if consensual, is a kind of annihilation. It is this trauma and the factors that forced it to happen that dovetailed with the traumas of my mother's life (and her mother's, father's, grandparents') and echo in mine. Colonization, both historical and ongoing, pulses throughout my body. Meanwhile, I stand facing the direction of my ancestors' homeland—east—listening for absent stories.

We tell our stories to convince ourselves of who we are, where we've come from. And if you're not able to access the resources—intact family lines, sane relatives, genealogical records, properly labeled family trees, history books in which you and your kind were written into the pages— or, alternatively, to speak the language your ancestors did and engage in traditional knowledge and practices, you're left with an accumulation of blanks, superficial displays you know better than to trust. I am magnetized to what is behind and beneath. I unearth with my pen.

I don't remember the details of any of my mother's weddings to all those white men. I don't remember the temporary relatives the men brought with them. I don't remember where or when they all disappeared, only that suddenly they were gone, not to be mentioned again, all evidence of them erased. Even the grief submerged. I remember my mother trying another church, the three of us daughters in tow. Fitted dresses that revealed her cleavage, her hair heated into looping waves, red lips and earrings that chimed as she moved. Jesus yet another man demanding devotion. I don't remember how many times I tried to learn Spanish to connect with my mother. The words in my textbooks were not the same as the ones she knew. I don't remember what she said to me the one time I tried to speak with her in public—only that I knew to never try it again. Whenever I invite Spanish into my mouth, my tongue thickens. My ears scramble what they hear. Is this my body remembering the nuns' punishment every time my mother spoke her language? Generations of the language native to the island, languages native to West Africa, suppressed within her. Her experience an echo of force controlling the voice, what was said and how. My tongue, my mouth, foreign when I mimicked her. The weight of wanting to speak what I could never get right. The heaviness of failure.

I don't remember how often I was left alone as a young person, both sisters having moved out as they neared eighteen. I was nine, and then I was eleven. I don't remember feeling lonely. I remember adapting to the torture of being isolated. At a certain point, I learned to take it with me everywhere I went.

———

I was fourteen when my mother first relaxed my hair. The scene could have been this:

"Careful of your eyes." She squirts perm solution on my hair, and instead of winding each section into plastic rods, as one would do to curl the hair, she spends half an hour watching me run a cheap black comb through it to undo the spirals I developed in early puberty. We're lucky to have the end unit of a two-story apartment building in Plain City, Ohio, my mother and I. That day, when we try to make my hair forget, we sit on a picnic table situated on the cement slab of our back porch.

"Keep it up," she instructs.

My arms are tired from the constant combing. The solution was not as toxic as what she used on her own coarse, tight curls. Her relaxer sat next to the bulk container of Vaseline under the sink, looming in its white plastic tub. The few times I screwed off the lid, a sinister burn cut through my nose and down my throat, souring my stomach. Monthly, she combed this white paste onto the densely coiled roots of her hair. It caked against her scalp. With a dish towel struggling to cover her shoulders, she would sip from a can of Michelob and eat handful after handful of salted peanuts as she sat in front of the TV until it was time to rinse out what erased the evidence of her. I'd seen it a hundred times.

"How much longer?" I ask.

It's evening, July 1991, the summer before my first year of high school. The same year in which the U.S.S.R. ceased to exist and the Paris Agreements allowed the UN to take over governance of Cambodia. Meanwhile, songs by Janet Jackson, Mariah Carey, Whitney Houston, and Gloria Estefan topped the charts—music that, for me, was mixed with 10,000 Maniacs' *Blind Man's Zoo* and Tracy Chapman's *Crossroads*. My initiation to protest songs that I could not yet make sense of but preferred to the songs on pop radio. Decades later in Loíza, I will learn that in the early nineteenth century, bomba songs seemingly speaking of love were actually protest songs, seeding fantasies of and directions for freedom. Just beneath tales of infatuation and plans for erotic encounters were instructions for how to escape, attempts to reunite family members who'd been separated by the slave trade.

In between more regular visits to the thrift store, my mother took me to Pier 1 Imports. In the early 1990s, their inventory included clothing, shoes, and accessories from around the world, primarily from developing nations, countries spanning Asia, Africa, Central and South America. A bohemian, global chic reflective of the 1960s counterculture explosion. I adorned myself with this imported clothing and was introduced to other versions of beauty. I never wore any of it beyond the confines of our home, caught between what was authentic for me as a changeling girl and what could be tolerated by others. Between wanting to celebrate what was truly pleasing to me as I got ready for school each day and being frozen in fear anticipating the reactions, the looks, the teasing, the racism, the threats because of my public display of identity.

My desire to wear bold tribal patterns, headscarves and hats, bright colors—ensembles of fuchsia, tangerine, and crimson, of turquoise, periwinkle, and cobalt—bangles and dangly earrings did not manifest. Instead, I wore black jeans and blazers, pulled my hair back, wore baby-sized gold hoops—a woman of questionable racial identity, subdued and in training. My mother utilized beauty as a kind of currency. It brought her attention, and, sometimes, power, disarming the mistrust engendered by her questionable origins, and gaining her inclusion. "You don't have to have money to have class," she often told me. Instructing me on how to behave properly, like a lady. I was taught to keep my appearance ambiguous: What *was* I? Where *was* I from? So long as I did not signal a particular race, I could benefit from my restrained personal expression. When I was wearing embroidered or beaded apparel, bright colors, large earrings, or bold lipstick, my café con leche skin tone, just like hers, stood out, thereby narrowing the possibilities for how I would be engaged with or treated. Many of my cousins—first and second—with their darker skin tones, did not have access to an ambiguous appearance. They did not have the choice to play a game that kept others guessing, a chance to betray themselves in the same ways I did.

High school did not feel far enough away from my first rides on the school bus and elementary school taunts. To those kids in rural Ohio in the 1980s, calling me an "Oreo" was meant to set me apart, call out my difference. I doubt they knew the conventional use of the label— Black on the outside, white on the inside. Rather it was a way of assigning a Black heritage that I didn't know how to acknowledge, let alone include, until it was done for me. The only colors available to them were white and black, and there was never a recognition that color could exist on a spectrum or have its own language, its own culture and cosmology, its own equal worth. That I was both was not a consideration, as if that would've made me closer to them somehow, closer to the belonging that

I, like any child, desperately craved. The freedom to play without being made to account for the way I looked or suffer the self-consciousness of wondering how others saw me. To them, my being Black meant not only that I wasn't like them but that I was less than them, an inherently impoverished version of a human who should be treated as such. White was the ruler against which all else was measured. There was white and the absence of white. I stood out in my difference, which made me an easy target worthy of ridicule. It was racist and cruel even for six- and seven-year-olds.

Despite a growing tenderness for and sprouting curiosity about my own difference as I crossed over from the territory of childhood into the borderlands of womanhood, I needed to look like the other girls. This did not happen, but I still tried. During summers spent sun worshipping alongside them. I was met with temporary admiration—oh, how I could keep browning—only to stand with them at night in the moonlight, in the company of boys we liked, and hear someone say to me, "You're so dark, I can only see your teeth." Quickly excluded for tanning too much. I was slow to learn and quick to forget these lessons. Wooed by the camouflage of friendship and the safety of inclusion only to be caught off guard when my difference was called out. I was not like them. I was not equal. I did not belong. Witnessing flashes of myself against the stark backdrop of whiteness both excited and terrified me. Invitations to access more of myself were a betrayal to what my mother insisted we strive for—to stay hidden in plain sight. In those small Ohio towns of my youth, the pretending acted as our salvation. So long as "other" went undefined and I was in my palest form, I could almost pass.

I will never really look like the other girls, but still, every month, Ma mixes the solution, douses my hair in it, and hands me the comb. By this time of day, in the waning hours of dusk, my mother has already held her hands above her shoulders for ten hours, cutting hair in her barbershop, both hands up as if she is in a state of constant surrender. Her shoulders and upper arms are mounds of strength. Tonight, for once, she does not have a date. She has me.

"How much longer?" I ask.

"Twenty minutes," she replies, as I continue tugging at the comb.

———

Two years earlier, during my first weeks in this new town and my new junior high school, my limbs extended, long and thin, as if plantlike, as my sisters' had. One day, I walked home with a classmate, another twelve-year-old, whose trailer park was down the road from our apartment complex. "Watch me," she'd said, pulling in the thin line of her bottom lip. "See if you can do yours like this." I mimicked her, gathering all that I could into my bottom teeth. "Yes!" she yelped. I had managed to reduce the size of my lips. I looked a little less like what I was, which to her was a triumph. The problem was that when I smiled, mirroring the attention and triumph back to her, I lost control of my lips and they spread, generously, revealing my large mouth and expansive grin. My inheritance—a mouth, jaw, teeth that will endure. Survive, as my Afro-Caribbean ancestors had survived. Disappointment passed over her face. "See how long you can do it for." As we continued our walk and she talked about what I cannot remember, I focused my attention on nodding at her and breathing through my nose, which made my nostrils flare (another corrective lesson), as I held in my lips. I did not know that what I felt—the inner lining of my skin shrinking away from itself and the head-to-toe burning and tightening—was the somatic expression of shame. A feeling, embodied. Instead, I just tried to get it right. It was the performance of an identity that did not belong to me. I had watched my mother do the same. Perform a kind of whiteness. Even though she didn't get it right, she never gave up trying to hide all that she truly was.

Three decades beyond this moment, I will learn from David Bedrick, esteemed author, counselor, attorney, teacher, and self-defined "psychological activist," as well as the founder of the Santa Fe Institute for Shame-based Studies, how much shame functions as a destructive force. One of the most impactful of his assertions is that "when shame rules, you stop feeling your profound connection with the human story and people around you. . . . Your world contracts as you learn to fit into a smaller and smaller space. In short, you become more alone."

There is a field behind our apartment complex, thick with stalks of feed corn. Beyond that, the Super Duper with its dirt-stained linoleum floors, rows of Wonder Bread, and spoiling meat; beyond that, hog farms; beyond that, the high school, surrounded by a sentry of heifers; and beyond that, nothing but sky.

My mother, with legs crossed, kicks her left foot against a white plastic pot of red geraniums—too many identical petals to count, but I try; anything to distract me from the constant combing.

Fans lodged in open windows above us hum. We hear a car roll down the alley, half a block away, its tires spitting gravel. A neighbor in the complex stands over a smoking charcoal grill. The smell of steak, denser than the Spam we fry, clouds the air.

"How much longer?" I ask again.

The weak picnic table swings at the release of her weight. She stands behind me, takes the comb, tugs it through my hair. With her free hand, she holds the side of my neck to help with the strain.

> **"You already stand out.
> Don't draw any more attention to yourself."**

I remember all the skin conditions of my teenage years. Regular trips to the dermatologist in a suburb of Columbus. The empty waiting room; framed prints of painted fields, Amish buggies, and sunsets; barely audible elevator music; a contrived tranquility that could not have been further from my own reality at the time. The chairs faced windows that looked out onto the street. I watched for the occasional tires passing, pairs of shoes, mismatched gaits. My mother had just married or was about to marry her fourth husband, against all my warnings. My older sisters had long since left home and were consumed with their own lives. The brunt of my mother's decisions landed on me. Womanhood seemed a punishment to endure. This is what I saw in my mother, who seemed to contort and shape-shift for the promise of love, only to unravel into a dormancy that left her in bed, minimally responsive, suddenly unbothered by the weight that began to pad her or her hair graying and tightening into its natural coiled state. Love didn't shine like the fantasy offered during courtship. Love had expectations, required participation, a vulnerability that I imagine confused, frustrated, and terrified her. Grief and depression, longing and abandonment threatened to drown her, so she gripped me, my life, my buoyancy. I was the one to keep her afloat.

In the dermatologist's office, I would squirm while I waited. Under the hyper bright examination lights, the doctor's pale, disinfected hands grazed the skin on my face. He vigilantly tested my blood for the antibodies that would force him to diagnose me with lupus. Something he didn't want to explain to me, didn't want me to learn about, didn't want me to scare myself with. *The body is constantly changing. Let's wait and see.* How I came to be his patient, how my mother could afford him, is beyond my knowing, but his wisdom and gentle demeanor and my mother's financial sacrifice for my care were all unusual gifts at that time. Perhaps because it was so undeniable, my condition. There was no hiding it. My face had lost pigment. Suddenly a question mark bleached across my right cheek and behind my right ear—vitiligo, which I fought with topical steroids. And the second diagnosis, pityriasis rosea—a rash extending across my back in the shape of a great tree. Every ancestor accounted for, not by name but in my very skin. The poetry of symbols.

The doctor's answer to our questions of why, how?

Stress.

In her prologue to *In the Dream House,* Carmen Maria Machado references Saidiya Hartman's essay "Venus in Two Acts," which explores the absence of firsthand accounts of slavery by enslaved people. Hartman uses the term "the violence of the archive," which Machado refers to as the idea that "sometimes stories are destroyed, and sometimes they are never uttered in the first place." While turning this over in my understanding, I consider how silence takes up space. I consider all its shapes.

The silence of rupture. The silence of protest. The silence of distance. The silence of waiting. How silence asserts itself, imprints on the body.

———

Throughout my early twenties, in a small, one-story home I shared with my husband at the time in Wooster, Ohio, I learned how to fill notebooks, to keep my hand moving. I learned how to sit in meditation on a zafu and zabuton, following one breath with another. I learned how to slow-walk, the steady placement of each foot, touching the trust implicit in the ground itself. I traveled to New Mexico and did this beneath Taos Mountain, at the home previously owned by Mabel Dodge Luhan, with a writing teacher, Natalie Goldberg. Her book *Writing Down the Bones* features timed units of freewriting with prompts such as "I remember," where first thought was best thought and the wild mind where these thoughts originated was prized. It became the way I confronted the blanks, my ancestors' and my own. With a fast-moving pen piercing the trauma, I felt it loosen its grip, lessen in power.

I existed.

I gave myself my existence as my hand traversed the page.

Here were my words, which came from my hand. I had a body. It was for me to fully occupy. Here was my mind; I observed it in ink. I could and did right/write myself back into my life. It started with the details of my body, sensory specific. It started with my voice reading what I wrote to others in the writing workshop, who did not comment, who only said, "Thank you." There was no space to deny or question. Only to listen, to receive.

There was so much to notice and catalog in those few weeks (a practice I have continued for over twenty-five years)—moments, memories, mundane details, a life being lived. With each page, I gave myself permission to take up space. I came to understand that I had a voice and that it was meant to be used.

What emerged in the space trauma had occupied? Connection to the core of myself beneath all the whitewashed layers. Then, connection to what was greater, to what moved in me with the sovereign knowing of my imagination.

Filling cheap spiral-bound notebooks became the way I proved to myself not only that I existed but also that I had a right to my story, no matter how much of it was missing and chaotic. I met my own mind. Writing became my practice. I learned how to make space for what happened when my pen crossed the page. My own presence meeting the unknown, the unseen. Penetrating beyond what I presented to the world about myself and about my place in it to the tender, hidden underbelly—raw, kaleidoscopic, inclusive truths I could claim. From here, I listened to what rose up to my awareness, touched my own lineage, getting at what was behind and beneath, to all those who dwelled within me: my constellation of origin. Story became my medicine. It narrated what I remembered and what I didn't remember. Trusting the threshold of formlessness into form, and cultivating unapologetic vulnerability, too, became part of my practice.

My notebook says it was like this:

In Old San Juan, in January 2010, the smells of sea, bird shit, and bougainvillea crowd the nose. In el Parque de las Palomas, you can buy a prayer amid a hundred pairs of wings. The density of waiting presses down on the tongues of the faithful, down on the backs of naked necks and knees, condenses on the eyelashes of los niños, who, looking across the water, see ghost ships and are reminded of masts and sails as they watch blouses, stockings, and slips anchored to lines suspended from apartment balconies. The bite of their madres', tías', y abuelas' stench— more pungent than detergent could ever hope to be—sailing, sailing, above it all. And las viejas praying, rosaries fluttering through their fingers, their lips becoming chapped as they plead.

Hurricane season is coming.

In the Plaza del Mercado, Angel and Jesus are just names. Dominican vendors. Hips bouncing babies. Cars scraping asphalt, begging to pass those in the way.

"Cómo? Cómo?"

Five-dollar perfume and high-heeled sandals in a bucket. Buy one pair, get the second for half price. A barbershop named Figuero. I attach an *a* to the end in my mind. Across the way, a pig's head, the size of a pumpkin, yellows in the butcher's window. Fruit falls from heaven and splits on the street. Husk. Skin. Seeds. Pulp.

I step around it.

People stand while they eat. Tilt away from the mess hanging from their mouths. Pigeons the size of cats strut on the curb. Constantly ripe, the body is waiting to open. It needs no instruction. Fifty miles below, I can only imagine the tectonic plates as they rub against each other. I can feel it all day long. The shifting.

Home is a question.

Flip-flopping through warm puddles in the streets of Rio Piedras, I pass my groceries from one arm to the other, the bag my own version of a heavy baby. I'm on my way back to my desk and my notebook, of course. Where I will list every detail. As I greet the ladies in housedresses, their damp hair rolled into curlers, and pass the boy on the other side of the chain-link fence—his lips puckered into one of the wire openings, calling for my attention—something occurs to me about the triptych of maps I taped to my bedroom wall five years prior when I moved to New Mexico.

What I had not asked as I studied the map of my family's origin was this: *Do you remember me? Do you remember my family? Even those who left? Even me, the first of those born off-island?*

And while I could not hear the answer, I could feel it as much as I could feel the generational scars of trauma from having to depart the island—for something better, which was better and not better. Where would it ever be better?

Years later, when I read Aurora Levins Morales's essay "Revision," I feel her words in my body, in my energetic roots—the potential of the profane, sovereign, and radical joy of being included claiming me:

Let's get one thing straight. Puerto Rico was parda, negra, mulata, mestiza.... All of us who are written down: not white. We were everywhere.... When most of the Indias had given birth to mixed-blood children, when all the lands had been divided, our labor shared out in encomienda, and no more caciques went out to battle them, they said the people were gone. How could we be gone? We were the brown and olive and cream-colored children of our mothers: Arawak, Maya, Lucaya, stolen women from the shores of the sea.... They called us pardas libres and stopped counting us. Invisibility is not a new thing with us. But we have always been here, working, eating, sleeping, singing, suffering, giving birth, dying. We are not a metaphor. We are not ghosts. We are still here.

———

I come from El Yunque pressing wet with life against my skin. Mud and waterfalls and orchids blooming in air. I come from the Great Mother, Atabey; from Guabancex, female deity of the winds; from Itiba Cahubaba, Earth Mother; and from Mamá Jicotea, Turtle Mother of all peoples. I come from fault lines rubbing deep beneath the sea, opposition that frictions into new land. I come from the river of beauty and love, Oshún; the ocean of motherly love, Yemayá; and the power of the wind, Oya. I come from the Island of Enchantment—the state of being under a spell—a place of magic. I come from the original people—worthy, honorable people—who had thriving systems. They did not go extinct. I come from what is beneath, what has been painted over—by assimilation, by time, by names, by the nature of graves, by colonization—and calls out in specificity. I come from the cobblestones in Old San Juan, taken from slave ships. I come from the backs that bent as they were put into place. I come from the sugarcane fields, lives stolen, sweetness stuck between teeth. I come from the simple freedom and magical suspension of a hammock; from chickens and horses wandering as they please; from sofrito, bacalao, plátano, cassava, arroz amarillo; from music demanding to be heard in ears and in hips every moment of the day and night. I come from the cacophony of being alive—yelling, dancing, crying, laughing, calling out to the next generation who pass by in diapers: Mami, Papi!

———

I remember turning eighteen and going to the Marion County courthouse with my mother and my tití to change my surname to their maiden name: Figueroa. After all, the only people I knew to count on up until then had been women. The only people I could relate to, did not fear, knew what to expect from were women. During my tití's visit, I was schooled on herbs. The uses and importance of manzanilla, a soothing plant taken orally or applied topically for insomnia, inflammation, ulcers, and wounds. We made tostones, plátanos flattened between cut paper bags after being fried once, and then fried again, dipping them in a tomato sauce with so much fresh ajo that I spent most of the night on the toilet. My aunt offering me cups of té de menta from the other side of the bathroom door. Garlic, a medicine to keep one's immune system strong, a natural antibiotic. Mint, to calm stress and anxiety and still a queasy stomach. My tití, a nurse devoted to her garden, who had always included the plants in her wellness practice, explained their uses to me.

I was just about to have sex for the first time. Another body entering mine seemed like one invasion I could control. As tempting as it was at times, I delayed it. I had watched my mother be taken over again and again, watched my sisters be taken over. The submission and the conquest in their love lives mimicked the gender roles they had been taught in their Evangelical church. I didn't want any of it and avoided church altogether and men for as long as I could. It's not that I hadn't been hurt by women, but that hurt was tolerable, familiar. Something I could anticipate and recover from. Men seemed inherently violent, untrustworthy, their fragility camouflaged and untranslatable to me. It was only a matter of time before they stole you away from yourself.

I don't remember the exact date we went to the courthouse, driving there or back, or the details of the courtroom the day we changed my last name. I want to say it was a cold spring day, overcast, but I wouldn't be surprised if I was wrong. I was raised by my mother; her sacrifices and her mistakes, her wounds and her wounding, her stories and the lack thereof were all that I knew. She was there. My father was not. That his name had anything to do with me when he hadn't earned it frustrated me. I ached for a sense of belonging to what was rightfully mine, a name that began to explain me and my family's story. Years later, on the island, I hear it is common for children to take their mothers' names. Claiming the matriarchal line is our traditional way. I come from women.

Ten years later, in another county courthouse, in Wooster, I will divorce my first husband: a hand-me-down version of one of my mother's—white and more than twice my age. It shouldn't be a surprise that I was in search of a father. Someone older and educated, who would protect me and teach me, who showed care. A trap of sorts set by the dominant culture, with all its patriarchal notions. At twenty-one, I willingly took the bait, was desperate to believe. I placed my foot on the trigger plate, the door snapped shut, and I gave up my freedom and my youth for something much more exotic and precious to me—consistency, predictability, stability, routine. The three-year-old in me, and the seven-year-old and the ten- and twelve-year-old, won out. Their needs drove my choice. Not unlike my mother.

Here was this man. This life. The restriction, for a time, was a relief. Until, of course, after some years I reached the end of the tether, couldn't tolerate the confines we'd agreed on any longer.

The courthouse was a grand space, with carved wooden benches; tall, imposing windows; and all the formality of a 1950s courtroom movie set. The judge, robed and seated on high, asked my plans. When I told him I was headed for New Mexico, the place that felt least like the U.S., where artists of all kinds metamorphosed, hippies and cowboys aged alongside each other, brown bodies were the majority, active Native communities asserted sovereignty, street names and surnames were in Spanish, and people shared a dialect hundreds of years old and an awe for the landscapes and unending expanses of sky—and where I'd touched the only sense of belonging I'd ever felt—he gave his approval that I was heading home. After all, my marriage certificate was from New Mexico. He could've also assumed this because of my last name and the way I looked: my summer skin and features; long, dark curly hair; embroidered blouse and jean skirt; dangly earrings and red lips. That Ohio was my official home, had been since my first memory, did not occur to him. It belonged to, was owned and ruled by, men who looked like him and my ex-husband. Still, I took his misconception as a blessing and drove cross-country with all that I could load into my old Subaru—my ex-husband kept the new one—looking forward to meeting the person, the writer, I had yet to become. Thankful that New Mexico would make room for yet another dreamer, yet another artist struggling to create their own way, exiled from another place, searching for rebirth. I followed the legacy of world-renowned writers and artists who had taken refuge there. "You can have me," I told the land when I crossed the state line.

There was a great love affair looming, with myself. My fantasies were all of her, writing. I wouldn't publish for another four years despite all the notebooks I filled and two practice manuscripts. It would be another sixteen years before I published a book-length work. All the while there was a slow becoming, my devotion to the practice of writing, and of reading and studying, of receiving life, of receiving myself.

———

Three years after my first trip home to Borikén, I returned with my mother, who had not been back in over fifty years, since she was sent away as a girl. I watched as she struggled not to be a tourist in her homeland. I watched the expressions on her face cycle between horror—prompted by a mix of tragic memories and internalized criticism of this place—to awe. What was the same as she had remembered it, what was not. Her Spanish in many ways frozen at the age she was when she left. Ghosts playing hide-and-seek.

At neighborhood cafés, everyone was Boricua. Families, individuals, teenagers, and elders, whether in swimsuits or business suits, each a unique expression of gender and class. She shook her head, straining to believe what was right before her eyes. Nothing to hide from, nothing to deny, nothing criminal, nothing wrong, nothing to be ashamed of, as she had continuously been made to feel. Only people. Human beings. Her people. Our people.

On public transport into San Juan, we were just another Puerto Rican woman and her daughter. At the beach, in the shops, in the museums, walking the streets holding hands. The experience touched generations of harm extending backward and forward, and that—*that*—was a kind of spiritual recovery.

I remember my mother's story. Told so many times it left me numb. Told to me when I was in my greatest pain. As if to compete and win the title of most aggrieved. To be honest, I have never let myself feel the entirety of my mother's story, to do so would mean surrendering to its possession, as she has done.

She was as young as six or as old as nine and had just arrived in New York City. Soon after, she was reunited with her older siblings and her parents. Her mother, Aida, took my mother shopping. She bought her a white dress with lace, black patent leather shoes, and white lace socks to match her dress. There were white gloves. My mother enjoyed the attention. She was clean. She smelled nice. Her hair was made to behave. Behold the sight of her. A wanted child. A loved child. Not a "throwaway child" as she would come to call herself well into old age. Her mother took her to the Mission of the Immaculate Virgin on Staten Island. In my mother's story, she is left on the front steps of the orphanage.

Her mother.

Left her.

There.

Where my mother cried all day and all evening until they took her in. She grew up in that institution, leaving only when she could make it on her own at barely eighteen. In exchange for food, clothing, a bed, and an education, she was given the Catholic variety of God, along with English—both forced. I have never seen a photograph of my mother as a child. The youngest I've seen her is at around nineteen in an army photograph. She had left the religious and educational institution of her youth for yet another institution—the military. It would behave in much the same way as the previous one, providing some things while violently stealing others, the least of which was innocence, an uninter-rupted connection with herself.

She was given away. She was left. She was not wanted. Her trauma, this trauma, formed a wound.

There have been times in my life when I knew this wound better than I knew her, than I knew myself. No matter the healing offered or the wealth of positive, wholehearted experiences she received—friendships, caring neighbors, church communities, the love of her daughters— the wound resurfaced over and over. Always ready to be activated on a moment's notice. Her power settled there, in that wound. It confined her. Who she was, who she could become, did not stretch beyond the wound's edges. Her family, the one she created by her own womb, the relationship with us, her daughters, and with her grandsons, was ulti-mately consumed by it.

That she was thrown away by those who brought her into the world, like the U.S. has thrown away and continues to throw away Puerto Ricans—island concerns, needs, and policies—makes visible a deplor-able and haunting parallel. The micro and the macro, the intimate and the unfamiliar, the internal and the external are stubbornly influenced. History is current and happening within our families, within our very bodies.

———

Shortly after turning forty and two decades of declaring writing as my practice, I felt an overwhelming desire to burn the notebooks I'd accu-mulated by diligently filling one a month. I had carried them with me from Ohio, and they'd since multiplied. With each move, chasing cheap rent from one side of Santa Fe to another, I stored them in sweater boxes beneath my bed, in stacking boxes in my closet, and, when I ran out of room, in the kitchen, in the bathroom. I had been reading them over time, which is also part of the practice Natalie Goldberg teaches in her books *Thunder and Lightning* and *Old Friend from Far Away*.

The days leading up to my former father-in-law's passing were there, in detail. The lamp in the corner of the room, a small constant light.

The tent formed by his large rib cage beneath the blanket. My mother's stay in a psychiatric care center. Her letters. A moment looking out the window. The many forms of a tree communicating sketched into words. Nights alone in the miniature apartment in a converted horse barn after I left my husband. My nephews' hands in my sister's garden, the ripening of a tomato beyond their palms.

It takes incredible effort to meet the details of a moment. It takes tremendous training to sit exactly where you are, hear only what you hear, be anchored in the now, follow first thought. It came and went in those pages, as did ramblings about worries and fears, both necessary and make-believe. The ways I could see myself. The ways I couldn't. Lines spoken by lovers; different lips, the same words. The ways they behaved like my mother. How it magnetized me to them. The dreams of losing my purse, my wallet, my ID again and again.

Nearly every day for a decade and a half ran through my pen, relived through writing, relived through multiple readings. I met myself, listened, understood, watched my patterns over the years, like a galaxy shifting.

I'd made notes, cataloged the notebooks by month and year, harvested poems, characters, stories. Before burning the notebooks, I considered ways of turning the pages into art. Could I sculpt a life-sized tree using them as papier-mâché? I had already used them to line cigar boxes and craft faux cigars for a performance piece in a local gallery. Could I use them as wallpaper? As insulation? Nothing ever came of these ideas. I ran out of space. And it was clear to me that I had fully claimed those moments and the person I had been, a version of who I was now. I had not wasted—I was not wasting—my life.

I called up comadres and rode into the backcountry of Coyote, New Mexico, to a fire pit. I wasn't the only one who had to cleanse and release my past. My sister-friends brought their versions as well.

What I didn't understand was how hot the fire had to be, how long it would take to convert pages to ash, given that the stack of boxes holding the notebooks was as tall as I was and twice as wide—quite the entity, born of my constant effort. Each page was proof of my existence, filled with realizations rising up from the dark interior of my brain, from the feral breath of memory, from my body. Each notebook was a blanket that I had wrapped myself in, that held me. I had found there what it meant to be "alone but not lonely." The blanket now a shroud. How long does it take for a body to be cremated? How hot is the fire? Wasn't that, in a way, what this was? The whole of my being. Trauma faced through the effort of somatic archaeology. Lifetimes cradled by my presence, funneling through me and burning in the flames.

There was a fondness for myself as if for an old friend, a part of me always bearing witness. This was why I had lugged the notebooks from place to place for nearly twenty years. Thousands of pages of blanks replaced by my own hand. There was gratitude and release. As we cara-vanned back into Santa Fe, we smelled of smoke and purifying herbs, our tongues tired as if we'd prayed for days. On my desk, in a small canning jar, sits a half cup of black ash and debris, one spiral binding, charred.

**"Don't trust those who are related to you.
Don't trust those who look like you."**

I want to say it went like this:

Our week together in Borikén had almost ended when my mother insisted that we pay an unexpected visit to her family's homesite and the legendary, feared cousins. After circling a neighborhood with unmarked houses for nearly two hours, passing the same group of children kicking ball, the same men sitting outside the bodega, the same chickens march-ing alongside the curb, the same woman with her calico bleached skin—vitiligo—on the porch of her mint-green-painted house with matching wooden shutters, flowers bursting from her yard, I tried to convince my mother it would not happen. That it was best to leave these people, our people, in peace. Everyone shook their heads when we asked about the address, gave them the names of our family. They didn't know us. They didn't know what we were after as we crept by in our rental car, relentless in our search.

One more time, she insisted. And around we went, again, the children, the men, the chickens, the woman on her porch. This time we included another street, where a woman inside a mess of a yard—trash and scraps of various kinds covering every square foot—tended to her cell phone.

My mother asked after her cousin, and the woman shrugged her shoulders.

"Park the car," my mother told me. "It's here. It has to be here."

Her audacity, intermittent and unpredictable, has always surprised me. Courage with a bite.

We found ourselves standing in the middle of the street in view of the last woman who'd rejected our request. Like many of the houses, hers was in a state of disrepair, surrounded by a high fence, and the gate had been wrapped in chains and padlocked. There was no way to knock on a door. We couldn't get that close.

My mother cupped her hands around her mouth and began to call the names of her cousins in a voice I imagine was the one she used as a child, before she left, before she was left, before, before, before.

"Pedro! Mateo!"

The woman continued to ignore us, but from the front door, a man appeared, darker than my mother but with similar features. As he unwound the chains and unlocked the gate, he smiled the same smile I see when I look at my mother, when I look at myself. Those teeth. That mouth. My inheritance.

The same woman who'd ignored us now gave a coy grin from her chair. The wife of my mother's cousin Pedro. Perhaps she had her reasons. I'll never know.

Out of nowhere, the past appeared in the form of my mother—long lost to the mainland—now an aging woman. Where would my mother's conversation with her cousin start? What would they choose to share?

"Prima! How've you been?"

Perhaps they had stories haunted with those who left and never returned. Another cousin appeared, Mateo, thinner than any man should be. The bones of his rib cage showing through his torn shirt. His feet bare. White hair and white teeth stark against his black skin. He opened a can of tuna and picked at it with his fingernails.

He seemed pleased to see my mother, and yet I believe we all could feel the decades, six of them, hanging over us like storm clouds, pressing down. Perhaps I was feeling tension, only a sensation, as I couldn't adequately get ahold of the conversation through the Spanish I barely understood.

Pedro brought out his prize rooster. It shone more gloriously than any peacock. As did he, when he embraced it.

My mother knelt at the feet of her uncle Manuel, our oldest living relative, for nearly an hour, flooded with a telling I could not comprehend. I tried to read her eyes, but they were too chaotic. He—along with his wife, my grandfather's sister—had cared for my mother and all her siblings when New York caught and reeled in her parents. There was an urgency in his voice, as if he'd been waiting for my mother's return to explain what had happened. It had the quality of a confession, his telling. My mother's mother had not been well in her mind. This was news to my mother despite it apparently being common knowledge.

Later, when my mother's eyes seemed to focus again, I asked her what her uncle had told her. After a long pause, she said that it was hard to understand him. That she couldn't grasp it all.

That she didn't remember.

Because I could see her distress and sense how tender she was, I did not ask again. Her emotional weight dragged her down, and I held her up.

This part of the trip is what stayed with her. It was all she recounted when asked about our time in Puerto Rico. While I was eager to share how wonderful it was to be "home" with her, her story was solidly in opposition. There was so much that went wrong. That was disappointing about the island, including me. The way I went into my room each evening and shut the door, keeping her out, away, keeping my distance. My attention on my notebook. That I didn't cook all her meals, that I didn't keep her entertained. The ways in which I left her alone.

———

I come from fragmented stories, trauma-splintered stories that are not mine to repeat—too much too much too much. I come from children who were abandoned again and again, who grew to be women. I come from women who were held down. Women who left their children and took in others. I come from women who fought back, who wielded knives, who shot guns. Women who escaped.

Wounded, wounding. Healed, healing.

I come from Taíno women and women from West African tribes. Brown-skinned and black-skinned women. I come from women who can lie so good, they can convince even themselves. Women who were remade, unrecognizable. Women who are scared of everything, including themselves. Women who have started over too many times to count. Women who have remained lost. I come from women who were deterred from their own wild knowing. Women who survived.

———

I come from.

I am from.

I am here.

I.

Am.

The woman who—by her own hand, through her ancestors' hands—is writing into her remembering.

"Those whom you love the most will abandon you.
You will find yourself again."

—JOY HARJO, *POET WARRIOR*

DISAPPEARED BY HUSBAND, PART I

LOOKING BACK NOW, DECADES LATER, I CAN SEE IT WAS A repetitive experience that happened in three stages. First, when she returned home with her soon-to-be new husband, my mother disappeared. Then, I was disappeared. Lastly, the men disappeared. Then the cycle repeated.

———

Do I begin with my mother's story, which mimics the fairy tale "The Red Shoes": "Once there was a poor motherless child who had no shoes"? Or do I begin with my own: Once there were three daughters, the youngest of whom endured her mother's dancing with a "hungry heart . . . terrible dancing [with] no rest"?

My awareness of our family bloomed in full color when I was around three. In that awareness, it is my two older sisters, my mother, and me.

Primarily, it is my mother and me. It is her body, her voice, her face, her attention where I find my belonging. All of this tells me I exist. She is mine.

The first night I spend away from home, at a neighbor girl's, I wake to the buzzing light of an aquarium. Fish with tails in motion, fluttering as if from the bottom of my dreams. Four years old, I let myself out the back door. The cool night air rises into the soles of my bare feet, gathers around my ankles. In the front yard of our duplex unit in Lorain, Ohio, I call out to my mother's open window on the second floor. It is not long before I see the lamplight, the silhouette of her hair, the reflection of her teeth as her smile widens. The front door opening, her arms, my home.

By this time, my mother has finished barber school, having graduated in the spring. Drizzle hung in the smeary blue night during our festivities. I can see the splinters of dark hair hidden in the creases of her blouse, in the pleats of her pants and around the stitching of her shoes. We, her three daughters, sniffed at her change. The success of her schooling was beyond us. What did we care about razors, perfect lines, a clean cut? She couldn't afford the life-sized mannequin head she was instructed to use for homework. This meant each of us had taken a turn serving as her practice model. We crowded around her, my eldest sister with feathered layers, my older sister with a Dorothy Hamill, and me with long bangs parted down the middle, each side held loosely in place with a barrette. We mimicked our mother's excitement. She was about to be licensed by the state of Ohio to cut hair!

On that wet spring evening, we'd propped the front door open, and the air snaked in thick and green. My mother turned on the stereo, her reward for having endured nearly a dozen years married to our father, Husband Number One, the weaponry of his words, the strike of a stiff, flat palm.

Kool & the Gang began to sing, "There's a party goin' on right here . . ." We did not know when she would begin her first job, which would mean more. More boxes of mac 'n' cheese, more Frosted Flakes, more Spam, a telephone that had a dial tone, and gasoline in the tank of the Buick. We did not know the importance of an education, or what "working poor" meant and how that term would define us.

Kool & the Gang harmonized the chorus, "Celebrate good times! Come on!," and we danced. We bounced and stepped, slunk low and twisted, shimmied and shook. The smiles we wore mimicking hers.

A Black woman from across the street stuck her head in the open doorway, her hair covered in a clear plastic shower cap. She sniffed at our party, eyed our mother. Her own children rushed in from behind her shadow, joining our dancing. She hung back, arms crossed over her loose, ample breasts, while we celebrated.

Celebrated what we did not yet have, what we hoped would come.

————

I have no memory of my mother's first marriage, the one to my father. He was a visitor. Their wedding is one I can only imagine.

In my mind's photograph, my mother's eyes are black plastic tokens that do not reflect the light, not the flash of the camera, not sunlight crossing the back of the empty church. Hers is a simple polyester dress, no buttons, no lace. Her entire body is the warm chestnut color of pantyhose, so she does not wear any. She is lighter than the Black folks her new husband's family knows. Her identity is questionable. They call her exotic. Her beauty and their ignorance converge. None of her in-laws from Henderson, North Carolina, know where or what Puerto Rico is. They do not know she warrants the pointed tip of racism, theirs. She is now his wife, an extension of him. They look at her as if she's a doll. She is as empty as the porcelain figurines on her mother-in-law's nightstand and only nineteen years old. Soon kicks will begin in her belly. Her groom has saved her from the army, from that officer. Never mind that there was no need and that his own kind of violence would soon follow.

My father wears his army uniform, medals earned during the Vietnam War pinned to his chest. Pale and good-looking, he can punch through thin wooden doors with his fists. In another photo, he is shirtless, holds a dead monkey upside down by its tail. Tropical forest threatens around him. He smiles. He is barbed wire and has a stomach full of fried potatoes.

My mother is a mere prize about whom he knows nothing, their courtship having spanned just weeks, but he promises, he says yes.

In her mind, he is everything she should submit to—golden. Her pass into places she could never go alone. She is from him now, no need to explain islands that may or may not exist. Her only experience of whiteness comes from the white bathtub in Heidelberg, Germany, where she will curl up while she swells with a dark-haired, fair-skinned daughter. For now, though, her lips are iced in pale pink. It is 1968. He hears the faint trace of an accent when she whispers. She only whispers. They stand side by side as if lining up for duty. Behind them tower shadows twice their size, waiting for them to turn around.

———

When I read Clarissa Pinkola Estés's rendition of "The Red Shoes," which she retells in *Women Who Run with the Wolves,* I am busy interpreting and assigning meaning. The circumstances of the destitute little girl in the story are not far removed from my own mother's experience as an island girl in poverty—suffering from diphtheria and tapeworms, foraging for ripe fruit, without enough clothing or any shoes, lost among many siblings and even more cousins. The wealthy old woman who takes in the little girl is represented by the Catholic mission where my mother was sent once on the mainland. The conditioning my mother received is similar to that of the little girl—her hair was "cleaned and combed"; she was dressed in "pure white undergarments," and made to look, think, and behave like those who forced her to submit, those who colonized her ancestors under the fifteenth-century papal bull *Inter Caetera,* which permitted the cross to function as any number of torturous weapons in the conquest of the New World.

How harsh is a punishment that deadens one's mother tongue? That makes one betray and despise all they are. That sees only the lack/

poverty and not the inherent value. That severs one from the ability to imagine one's own humanity and dignity.

The red shoes are the love and belonging my mother desired, the attention she craved, the longing for a vibrant, enlivened existence, one of being acknowledged, included, and cherished. Nothing wrong with that. Not even for a poor, undereducated, Spanish-Afro-Taíno child from an island owned by the U.S. government, no matter what the dominant culture said or continues to say. But in the story, when the little girl wears her red shoes to church, unbeknownst to the blind old woman, and passes by the odd soldier standing just outside the doors with his "little jacket" and "red beard," the first of three encounters throughout the story, the shoes become possessed, and what follows is a perversion of what was once pure. Some may think the soldier who turns the shoes into demented creatures that cannot be removed is the devil. The devil or, perhaps more accurately, the patriarchy, the puppet strings of empire.

And then we were leaving Lorain. It could've happened like this:

Giant black trash bags piled in the back seat of my mother's two-door Buick. Everything that could have used a box—spoons, sheets, clothes, towels, hairbrushes—stuffed into the trash bags, the bags' flaps tied into rabbit ears. I bounce around on top of them as we drive away from government housing, down streets filled with mothers and their children. Brown and Black mothers and their children. The last time this majority will exist for us.

My sisters and I were never properly introduced to Husband Number Two. If we were, I don't recall it. I recall only the movement. Driving away from the place that housed us while our mother went to trade school and learned to cut hair, practicing on us until she mastered, with perfection, the hairstyles of the late 1970s and early 1980s. Driving away from the only street I had ever known, the only families I had ever known, overflowing with women, round and fierce, who were the heads of their households, where men were rare and odd like jewels, too expensive to accessorize with and not practical, certainly not to be trusted, and not for keeps.

The streetlamps circle wide mouths of light into the dark car, illuminating my perch. I grip the rabbit ears of the shifting trash bags. We are leaving the beginning, mine, the one I remember. The place where my mother and sisters and I all slept in the same bed, our long brown limbs overlapping and intertwined, our breath moist and clouding each other's faces. The place where we paraded around without clothing, because it pleased us. We did not know there was anything wrong with our behavior, with our bodies. There was no one who would cut us a glance and punish us into hiding. In that duplex, paid for by welfare, we sang and danced to all the best disco on the radio, played maria-chi music on eight-track tapes left over from another time in Texas, the place of my birth, laughing as loud as our bodies were able. We were without the law of men, without the house laws of white men, but that was about to change. We were headed into a different reality, only an hour's drive south.

———

The excuses were written on half-torn pieces of lined paper ripped from my notebook, the shaggy ends evidence of her hurry. The date in the upper right-hand corner. One simple sentence slanted in my mother's cursive. No matter what grade I was in, or how long I'd been absent, it never changed. Not one time in twelve years of schooling. "Jamie was absent [was tardy, must leave early] due to uncontrollable circumstances." Her signature in the lower left-hand corner, her last name dependent upon which of the five men she was married to at the time. Beneath her signature in parentheses, the word *mother*. All those times holding the slip in my hand and passing it to the school secretary, I never thought to ask my mother why this phrase, nor did I think to have her change it; instead, I simply felt relief for the time away from classes and peers and the embarrassment of having a mother who seemed to know only how to do one thing and keep repeating it.

———

I overheard my mother talking on the phone while she was in the initial weeks of her marriage to Husband Number Two. "He treats me like a queen," she'd say in a tone that seemed both deserving and surprised.

I wasn't sure what that meant, exactly. Of course, I was familiar with the queens in storybooks, none of whom looked like my mother. Alabaster white and pale eyed, modest yet ornate. If there was a queen, then there was a king. In all royal logic, that made us, her daughters, princesses, but that seemed so unbelievable it was comical, or cruel, depending on which position of the court one held.

My mother's room with her new husband was in the upper reaches of his split-level home. My own bedroom was on the ground floor, beneath the living room and kitchen. Next to my door was another one that opened to a staircase descending into the basement. An unfinished, cold, dark space with cement floors and bare light bulbs fixed to the rafters. I avoided it. It terrified me, seemed too large. The whole house terrified me. Too many levels, sets of stairs, rooms—endless rooms with seemingly endless shag carpeting.

I was alone at night for the first time. I could feel the animal hunger of my body for the bodies it knew in order to sleep. To dream.

Not long after, I began to sleep with my eldest sister, who tolerated me as a second mother would. Crowding her were smells of oily skin and hair, and the sweet/sour of rising bread. Her back broken out in acne, the skin textured with scars, hard and soft pimples, like mine would later be as well. She was a freshman in high school; I had just begun the first grade. There was enough of a difference in our ages that she was able to provide kindness and comfort in the absence of our mother, whom I rarely saw before leaving for school, who would still be at work when I returned home. Once she'd finished her long hours in her barbershop, she'd be quickly ushered by the king into their bedroom. The door was always shut. Locked.

On occasion, we were allowed to join them in their room, where a small TV sat on the expanse of his dresser. Piled between the wooden headboard and footboard, all of our girl limbs reaching for our mother nearly drowned him. A look of tolerance stained his face. His three children were grown and lived on their own. He was older than my mother by some years, his hair and beard were variations of white and silver, his face wrinkled and worn into shades of pink. He fit the part of the king—bloated with alcohol, teeth stained from nicotine, a commanding voice, rules, laws, and decrees of all kinds. I noticed his shoes in the closet, leather and shiny, each one ornamented with a tassel; in the laundry basket his large white square briefs, a thick band of elastic around the top; the five-gallon glass jar full of coins in the corner of their room. Pennies, mainly, but buried here and there something silver catching the light.

Clearly, they had dated, and then there was an engagement and a wedding. Perhaps even a honeymoon. But I don't remember how they met. Nor do I recall him coming by. There had been another man I had been fond of who brought me small stuffed animals and had long, wavy, dirty blond hair, but he already wore a wedding band.

The husband did not exist, and then he did, and we were moving in with him.

There was a willow tree nearby—perhaps it was in our front yard or the neighbor's—which I drifted to when waiting for the school bus full of white children who would repeatedly question my race, call me out as different. Were they able to see me better than I could see myself? There was a way in which I relied on them to define me, a budding self-betrayal. I despised them for the power they had and the loyalty they demanded, and that I gave them, feeling an unnameable lurking heaviness—the guilt of a traitor outsourcing their authority. They didn't wait for me to answer, because it wasn't a question, it was an accusation. I was not like them. I was not white.

I didn't know how to answer. How would I defend myself—what was my defense? Their taunts stung. I felt bad, wrong, distracted by trying to comprehend what others saw when they saw me. Even my own mother, when asked what I was, would laugh and say, "Heinz 57," as if I were just a long list of ingredients. She didn't once say, "My daughter; we are Boricua/Puerto Rican, a mix of Afro-Taíno and Spanish ancestry." Or, "Her father is of Irish descent. That's what you see when you look at her." I'd like to think that if my mother had said this—or something, anything—I would have felt some semblance of ground upon which to stand. But that act of claiming her own identity, and teaching me how to claim mine, was beyond her. The nuns had made sure of that in their punishments, in their acts of assimilating her. And the layers of over-culture, first American and then "Hispanic," both of which reinforced white as better, lighter as desired. Protecting her daughter meant shield-ing her from who and what she was, who and where she came from. It was a confused, perverse protection that favored others and assuaged their concerns, that took care of them instead of me.

Weekly, her husband held "family" meetings where, as king, he would restate the rules, list our criminal deeds, and then offer up the floor to anyone who had "gripes," which I heard as "grapes" and sat on the couch in a mess of emotions, trying to sort out the connection between fruit and the pain on my sisters' faces, the tears my mother quickly wiped away when she was prohibited from coming to her daughters' defense. I thought of the green and purple wax grapes my mother used to put in the center of our table before we'd gone to live with the king, along with an apple, banana, and pear—all wax. Our cupboards and refrigerator were scant with food, but fake abundance decorated the table where we often went hungry.

We were to call him not by his name but instead "Dad." We were not permitted in certain areas of the home. We were to leave our bedroom doors open. There was a strict curfew. Noise was an issue; our music—Stevie Wonder, Michael Jackson, Prince, Donna Summer—no longer sounded from the speakers. Dancing, and the easy, natural way it took over our bodies, was a problem. There was to be no snacking, ever. All food was heavily regulated—nothing was to be thrown away. Sometimes he would produce the last few bites of a sandwich, or some other wasted morsel covered in dust, specs of tissue, and hair from the bottom of the trash and set it on the coffee table during these family meetings. We would not be dismissed until one of us had confessed. Not surprising, then, that when our turn came to "gripe" at him for all that we did not approve of, it was strangely quiet. The clock's hands firing off a sound

at every minute. Cars passing by on the street. A dog barking. The snif-
fling. Vacant eyes directed at the carpet. No one in that living room was
present, beyond the mass of our physical bodies, except him. Each gone
to our respective fantasies. Magical thinking an escape that allowed us
to hover near our bodies without having to feel the full impact of his
violence. The separation from our mother, from each other. The disin-
tegration of family as I'd known it. Interrupted by the authority of this
man and his harm.

———

There were dead things for the first time. His son, the prince and treated
as such, would visit and gift me the tails of rabbits or squirrels he'd
hunted, which I would rub between my fingers and against my cheeks,
not thinking about where they came from or the bit of bone I could
sometimes still feel hidden inside. For the winter months that we lived
there, I had to walk by a doe hanging from her hind legs in the garage
on my way to the back door. Her tongue, eyes, nose, and ears turned
into accessories instead of the tools for survival they once were. I fixed
my gaze to the oil stains on the garage floor as I inched around her head
to grab the handle of the door. I held my breath in fright and squeezed
past, sometimes brushing up against her hide accidentally. She towered
over me, draining blood. It had been a fierce winter, and the garage was
a freezer, too cold for me to smell what was dead. Stretched the way she
was, she appeared taller than any man I'd ever seen, her weight straining
the rope.

I did not know my mother could shoot a gun. I did not know she
knew how to kill. I can still hear her laughter, not gleeful, but close,
when she was praised by the king for her hunting abilities.

His home is where I remember first being beaten with a belt by my
mother, although it could have happened before. But he was close by,
and the look on his face after it happened, the way he held his body—
chest puffed, arms crossed with fists in elbows, neck cocked—told me
that he, too, had somehow participated.

In her modern-day application of "The Red Shoes," Dr. Estés highlights the role of "hambre del alma," which she explains as "the starved soul . . . relentlessly hungry," writing, "A woman who is starved for her real soul-life may look 'cleaned up and combed' on the outside, but on the inside, she is filled with dozens of pleading hands and empty mouths. In this state, she will take any food regardless of its condition or its effect, for she is trying to make up for past losses."

I gave my mother regular detailed reports. I'd dash into the bathroom before she shut the door, and as she sat on the toilet, I'd recount every moment I'd heard or witnessed in her absence: conversations the king had on the phone, with neighbors, with his own adult children when they visited. What he said about her, what he said about us. The weight and responsibility, the pride, of rescuing this poor woman and her children, her three daughters in need of a father. His sacrifice. His generosity.

We survived three seasons in his home, far enough away from our mother that it felt like we existed in other countries, other kingdoms, other realities.

When the yelling began to seep from their chamber walls and floor, radiating throughout the house, my mother started attending a Church of Christ. The small congregation had taken over an old multitiered dinner theater with three separate sections that faced the stage, or pulpit of sorts, where the pastor—a wiry, pale, small-framed man with slicked black hair, dense and wavy—rolled up his sleeves and with a twinge of a Southern accent and an occasional but reliable giggle, delivered God's word. He was a storyteller. This put me in a state of awe. Never mind that his wife was irritated by my questions—*What about all the other gods? Why don't we talk about them?* Even at six years old, I knew better than to trust a monotheistic faith. I had not been exposed to expressions of the Divine Feminine, but this was what naturally constituted my first ideas about the Sacred. Before I had been taught otherwise, what I saw when I saw "God" in my mind's eye was a gathering of goddesses. I could feel the pressure of the pastor's wife, the use of dogma to attempt to control my mind, my heart, my soul. My innocent childish notions were pagan ideas, heathen, and needed to be corrected.

The assistant pastor, a Black man—the only one in the church—was a former boxer who towered over the pastor. He could outlaugh the pastor during guest sermons. I could hear him singing (all hymns were sung a cappella) above anyone else. I remember both men's arms. The short-sleeved dress shirts that left the bulk of their biceps and the cabled strength of their forearms in full view. They were workingmen.

My mother had the witnesses and the refuge she would need once she decided to escape. One day, the pastor and assistant pastor appeared at one of the king's weekly meetings and took turns talking to and listening to everyone in the house. Even us. After the family meeting, we were instructed to wait in my older sister's room, where we sat on her bed in a semicircle. Posters of boy bands looking over our shoulders as the two pastors eventually joined us and listened as we listed the ways we'd suffered. The evidence of some, they could see. The lack of phones except in the master bedroom. The ways in which we would slink from wall to wall, puddle in corners to avoid "Dad," for fear of doing something, anything, wrong. The longing we felt for our mother on the other side of the couch, beyond the moat.

The king was eventually permitted to join us, the pastor and assistant pastor flanking him. He was made to apologize to us, and he did, on his knees. It was a performance I enjoyed very much. In addition to the apology, there were promises. A trip to some impossible place. Florida? The beach? Disney World?

When he left, I turned to my eldest sister, my face full of hope.

"Did you hear what he said?" I asked her, ready for everything to be instantly better.

Without hesitation, she replied, "You don't believe him, do you?"

Her rightness, which would soon become clear, was so sharp and unexpected that I can still feel the cut of it now. How could I have been so stupid as to think that a man, this man, could change?

———

It's the motion I remember. The adrenaline. The desperation. Leaving. I always remember the leaving. A cigar box crammed with bloody fish heads delivered to our door for him to open, left on the porch step. Who had sent it? The pastor? The assistant pastor? Later, I overheard a conversation from a corner in the pastor's kitchen, but I couldn't decipher exactly who'd done it.

Then there was the end.

My mother couldn't seem to sit still the days before it happened.

———

I remember it this way:

Gravel. The dark. Three pairs of feet, four including mine. My mother's beat-up yellow flats chewing the driveway. Her short brown legs in the headlights. The car's interior light, dim and flickering. Our getaway car, our constant, the two-door maroon Buick. The felt from the ceiling sagging. I hadn't known what to grab when my mother said to take only what mattered. My hairbrush, a copy of *Jumanji* I had borrowed from the public library and never intended to return, a drawing I'd done the week before of a swan, a Little Debbie snack cake I'd saved from a visit to a neighbor girl's house.

My mother and my sisters scrambled around me in the dark. Ma's curler set, our shoes, various items of clothing were passed in bundles and relayed from my eldest sister to my older sister on the lawn to my mother's waiting arms a few feet from the car. When the trunk was filled, she threw what was left in armloads onto the floor of the back seat.

He'd gone to the store. He was the one who did the grocery shopping. The cooking. It was his house, and he controlled such things. My mother spoke a few words in Spanish that had become obsolete to us by then, in Canal Fulton, Ohio, but on that night under her breath—

"Ándale."

I didn't know if she was talking to us or to herself, but we could not have moved any faster. I had been used as a sweeper, collecting the crumbs of socks, spoons, and cheap perfume bottles—nearly empty—until I tripped on the front cement stoop, knocking out a tooth. It was already loose, but still it bled enough to scare us all. My mother dropped the twelve-inch TV set she had lodged beneath her armpits, snapping the antennae off the back, and scooped me up, carried me to the back seat, her heart a hurricane against the shore of her sweaty chest, whispering,

"Ándale. Ándale."

Then, a car engine and the sound of gravel growing louder, as my sisters abandoned their posts and dashed for the car. My mother rescued fallen T-shirts and windbreakers strewn across the lawn. My eldest sister's compact mirror cracked on the rocks, her other makeup spilling from her pillowcase as she tried to grab it.

The boat of his Lincoln docked behind us, blocking us in. Ma in the headlights of both cars. His hands in the air as if fighting off bees. The way she gripped the mismatched socks to her throat as if they would protect her.

The sound of panting we all made in the car, as if we were collectively one prey. We never would have been allowed to leave. But we were in the car now, and the neighbors were within earshot. The limbs of the willow tree where I'd often waited for the bus shimmered in the headlights as if silver rimmed, swaying against the ground. My secret of safety, the only thing I would miss.

———

The notes were sometimes torn, a corner missing, the bottom edge uneven. There was no well-intended presentation about them. "Uncontrollable circumstances." It was a formality. Perfect attendance, while prized by some of my peers and rewarded by teachers, was never something I even considered possible. Perfect attendance accompanied other routines that were not a part of my daily life—meals around a table with family members, consistent hygiene, parental participation in school activities, supervision of schoolwork and the phases of my childhood development, regular guidance on how best to navigate the overwhelming jungle of existence. Our lives raged outside the confines of the school. How could I keep up with anything else? Attendance was required by the government. I'd heard about truancy officers. Sometimes warnings about excessive absences were sent home, but I wasn't concerned. School, and all that it entailed, was a kind of fiction. I had my mother's handwritten notes. My ever-applicable excuse.

I hold the memory close as if it were this:

I watch my mother's body while the pastor shouts from the pulpit, squeezes his last bit of breath out into a sentence that leaves him on his toes, the veins in his neck visible. Faith. A mustard seed. In another church, sunlight burns through glass. In another church, Mary, with her head down, all those sheep. In another church, the air is stale. The wooden pews force us to pay attention.

I watch my mother's pulse. It throbs in the cup of her neck. With my index finger, I trace the veins crossing the backs of her hands as if I'm placing them there.

There is no God I can comprehend—another white man demanding devotion—only the skin of my mother, her steady quiet breathing.

One word transcends: *creator.*

When alone and temporarily uncoupled, my mother got closer to an expression of herself that I could recognize. Uncensored. Unleashed. Her body made noises. Her laughter tore through our ears. She had something to say about everything, about anything, whether it was correct or not. She was not acceptable. She was not polite. There was no hesitation between what occurred to her and what she voiced. Bedroom doors and bathroom doors always open. The binding of clothing rejected—

blouses hung unbuttoned, bras were undone, zippers gaped open, pants fell away like petals unpeeling. Her hair closer to its true state, her face free of makeup, her body reeking of musk, her feet bare and resting on any surface. By herself, she seemed to swell within our apartment, and we attached ourselves to her warm flank. While her moods could and would still fluctuate, at least we were close. We held her, and she held us.

———

I remember it like this:

Sitting at our round kitchen table, a plain cloth covering its dark lacquered wood, a small rectangular can of sardines in front of my mother. In our own place after taking temporary refuge on the couch and floor of the pastor's house for some weeks. I could still conjure in the back of my throat the taste of Kool-Aid made with well water from the pastor's tap. Iron-rich, like blood.

It was almost summer; both the front and back doors were wide open. My eldest sister and older sister walked on their thin, long legs, wobbly with impending womanhood, through the kitchen, excitement sparking off them. Something about boys, a new song on the radio. I didn't know that fish lived in cans, but there they were. Packed side by side, a crowded puzzle of bodies, shiny and silver, like a collection of pocketknives. My mother dipped her fingers in and pulled one out by the tail fin. Inserted it into her mouth and began to chew. I heard it crunch. With each fish she ate, low moans of fulfillment rose from her.

Did I want one? She held it up between her forefinger and thumb.

I looked at the metallic sheen of the scales, the flat black eyes smaller than beads, and shook my head. Everything was suspicious: the fish in a can, my mother's fingers pinching each one and dropping it into her mouth, the sound they made being pressed between her teeth.

"I'll give you a dollar"—she sucked oil from her bottom lip—"if you eat one."

She pulled a bill out of her purse and laid it flat on the table, a green paper serving platter for one single sardine. She fished out the longest, most plump. Lifted it into the air and dared me again. There was a list forming in my head of what I could buy with the money: Little Debbie snacks, crayons, paper.

The sardine wouldn't have fit into my mouth head to tail. I would've had to bite it in half. My teeth severing its malleable rib cage, just below its currant-sized heart.

I pinched the soft skin of my mother's bare legs, snuggled into her armpit. Surely, she would give me the dollar without me actually having to eat the fish. She waited for my answer.

My sisters had stopped to watch, pawing at the carpet with their thin toes, their eyes wide. Even the fish seemed to be waiting for me to decide. I buried myself deeper into my mother's torso, mumbled into her breast.

"Can I just have the dollar?"

She stood, fingers covered in oil, stuffed the dollar bill back into her purse. The sardine left on top of the others, diagonal, instead of aligned in its perfect puzzle fit, a slippery little beast. My mother, a mystery to me.

When courtship descended, after self-help books were tossed under the bed and love songs repeated, each time louder until they made my stomach flip, churn with nervousness and dread, her dancing took on a different series of steps—frenzied, desperate. We knew it was only a matter of time before a man would darken our door, and in his presence would be a variation of her, the slightest one possible. Perhaps the one that she thought he could tolerate, that would still earn her his attention and love. Her self-reduction was so thorough that I could be sitting across from her at the table with the man of the moment and have no idea where she was, where she'd gone. Only a flash now and then from behind her eyes, as with anything wild and caged in a state of momentary submission.

"The problem with the girl in the red shoes is that instead of becoming strong for the fight, she is off in la-la land, captured by the romance of those red shoes," Dr. Estés explains in her extensive unpacking of "The Red Shoes." "The important thing about rebellion is that the form it takes be effective. The girl's fascination with the red shoes actually keeps her from a meaningful rebellion, one that would promote change, give a message, cause an awakening."

———

My sisters and I had returned from spending the summer months in Massachusetts with my father's family—his second wife and young children, as he seemed to be gone for weeks on end—to find our mother distracted by someone she would soon couple with and marry. Husband Number Three. Again, she was an arm's length away in his presence.

There had been benefits to a summer away—I'd learned to ride a bike, finally, at eight years old; I played outside every day with the other kids my age on the street, in expansive backyards; meals were regular, and there was enough to eat; there were morning and evening rituals, supervised by my stepmother. I was made to brush my teeth, and I slept with my younger half sister in her canopy bed with frilly bedding, amid her white matching furniture and abundant supply of toys; I fed my younger half brother slices of Kraft cheese, his toddler hands waiting while I unwrapped the plastic and handed him the sheet of processed orange each day like a pet in training.

There was a series of near disasters—the fighting between my father and his wife when he was around; her nights on the front steps drinking from a bottle of wine until her speech became slurred, her balance precarious as my older sisters escorted her inside; the neighbor boy who insisted on scaring me with his penis from behind his screen door; my sisters' separate and faraway lives with boys who drove cars and the room they shared, where they played Madonna's new album, *Like a Virgin;* the bike crash where I blacked out and woke to an older German woman carrying me home, comforting me in her mother tongue. And the day before we left, gripping my father from the back of his motorcycle, sans helmet, in tears after he told me I was never going home, would never see my mother again. He waited until near bedtime to take

it back. But the distrust of him I developed in those moments continued and has remained.

Husband Number Three, on the other hand, was different. He was
soft-spoken. He had red hair, was fair and freckled. His side part was
consistent. He didn't seem to need all the attention anyone in his presence could offer. He listened more than he spoke. It was often quiet
around him. He smiled easily, a conservative grin, the edges of his lips
slipping upward. His jokes were gentle, and he didn't tease. He had a son
and a daughter, I believe, close to the ages of my sisters. If I had to make
up how he and my mother met, it would be that he'd come to service her
telephone line at our new duplex, as he worked for Ohio Bell.

––––––

Memories of him go like this:

Getting fat together, buffets after church, all-you-can-eat, the relief
for a time of not being hounded by hunger. My mother filling glass jars
with rice and beans of all colors, shapes, and sizes. My mother softening
and quieting, something inside her sated and asleep, making sourdough
bread from a starter that sat on the kitchen windowsill. Another duplex,
one that we all shared, on Redwing Drive at the end of small-town neighborhood construction where the forest gathered behind our back door
and I would play for hours, my hands and feet covered in leaves and
twigs and mud, until my mother whistled for me with her whole hand
in her mouth, a call I knew. My older sister complaining that I smelled
like a dog, reeking of sweat and earth. On days I didn't go outside, I'd
curl up next to him and my mother on the couch, where we'd melt away
in front of the TV. On my ninth birthday, I hosted a sleepover party, a
first and last, where my friends and I played *Star Search,* a microphone
attached to my boom box as I squeaked along with Whitney Houston,
my long hair swaying against my back.

We took a trip, a family vacation, the three of us, him, my mother,
and me, to Canada, where we stayed for what in my memory feels like
weeks but was, in reality, most likely a long weekend. My sisters must
have stayed with friends, or perhaps they were permitted to be home

unsupervised as they were both old enough to drive. A vacation was something entirely foreign, and even though the cabin was modest, to say the least, as was the fishing boat we took out every day, there was an easiness to being together. Our simple relaxation had a rhythm. I drew or read on the water all day while they pulled up dinner on the line. My mother cleaned and fried the fish—yellow perch, northern pike, walleye, trout. There is a photo of me holding up a line in each hand, six fish hanging on either side of my small torso. I am straining under the weight, but my smile is abundant, fierce. We told stories and jokes and then shared a bed. Him, my mother in the middle, then me. Him calling out a mosquito warning in the dark: "747, incoming!" The mattress shaking from our combined laughter. He was calm, and my mother seemed calm around him—for a time.

But back in our duplex during the following months, I'd find her in the basement, beneath her plastic helmet dryer, hair stretched over large rollers, smoking cigarettes, biting her nails, near tears. Her calm became disturbed. There was a slow-growing dissatisfaction. Any trace of her discontent vanished when she emerged onto the main level. We had a cat, the first of several who would get sick and die unexpectedly or disappear. Decades later, the same would happen to a series of dogs. At first obsessed with a pet, my mother would eventually lose interest, then neglect it. Soon thereafter, she'd give it away or it'd come up missing, dead. Only to be replaced by another.

At school events, class plays and choral performances, it was Husband Number Three whom I would find in the audience waving at me. It was Husband Number Three who played catch with me, who attended my softball games. Who made me fried cheese and who created a buffer from the harms of life, provided consistency and predictability amid my mother's emotional torrents. If I were to call any man "Dad," it would be Husband Number Three. Not my own father or Husband Number Two, who had demanded it. In the three years they were together—spanning the start of my seventh year well into my tenth—he was steady, routinely navigating my mother's storms. Her excitement, her obsession, her boredom, her listlessness, her withdrawals into silence. The push and pull of her.

When Husband Number Three got a job promotion, we moved hours south to a suburb of Columbus. Was it six or nine months later that my mother's dancing consumed her, the sickness returning? Showing up alone at parties my school friends' parents hosted, her hair whipped into dark waves, her cleavage on display, red-lipped, wearing chandelier earrings, her perfume infesting each room where she lingered. The staring, the stares. Too many drinks, the car ride home, her fighting to keep to her side of the center line. Me vigilantly watching in case I needed to grab the wheel or warn her of what she wasn't paying close enough attention to. Her eyes. The blue contacts she'd given herself at Christmastime. What did she see when she looked out of them? When she looked at herself in the mirror, as I would see her doing, had she become someone else? Was it who she wanted to be?

Eldest Sister enlisted in the army so she could get money for college. Her calls from boot camp shook us. She was always crying, her wailing muffled by the receiver against my mother's ear. Perhaps this disturbance unsettled my mother's memories of her own time in basic training. In the army, before any assault from an enemy force, there is the potential of assault from the men in one's own unit, including one's superiors. That my mother could not protect her daughter from violence, as she could not protect herself, seems an old, old tale that has been repeated for centuries.

Older Sister counted down what remained of high school, as the move had impacted her social standing. She'd gone from being the beautiful, popular freshman elected a homecoming attendant at a small rural school—perched on the back of a Corvette convertible wearing her sash, in a parade around the football field with others who'd been voted on to the court, the senior king and queen—to just another girl in a class of hundreds. It is hard to locate her in my memories during this time. She worked at Kentucky Fried Chicken and saved enough money for an old beater that she drove to a trade school miles away in the flat, corn-filled expanse to study cosmetology.

Husband Number Three came undone at my mother's regression, the way in which she distanced herself from him. His pain, his grief while she gathered all her love and took it back. I felt the coldness of confusion in my veins, sharp edges of anxiety, nervousness and dread threatening to slice me from the inside, until the numbing began, and I froze over.

Then he was gone.

And we were moving, again.

"When a woman is unconscious about her starvation, about the consequences of using death-dealing vehicles and substances, she is dancing, she is dancing. Whether these are such things as chronic negative thinking, poor relationships, abusive situations, drugs, or alcohol—they are like the red shoes, hard to pry a person away from once they've taken hold," writes Dr. Estés in *Women Who Run with the Wolves.*

My mother disappeared men. Men whom she'd welcomed into our family and demanded that we welcome, too. Sometimes we did, but it didn't matter. In the end, when she was finished, they went away, or we went away. It didn't matter if the men were cruel or kind. If they deserved such punishment or not. They were treated the same. After all, they were only screens onto which my mother projected her ideas of a man, her desperate needs, her past hurts, her longing—ideas of love manufactured by mainstream movies and commercials, a constant supply of never-ending images of a normal that ever escaped her, that dogged her.

The leaving was thorough and severe. It was rare that the men were

ever mentioned again. The memories accumulated in their company—
thrown out. Those shared years of our lives—discarded.

Disappearance and death registered as the same in me. If I no longer see you, no longer hear you, no longer know you, if no one talks
about you or remembers you, you do not exist. Did you ever? Did I
make you up?

———

While there were many boyfriends and many evenings my mother went
for a drink at some nightclub, two men are distinct in my mind. They
could not have been more different. Clowns, however sinister, in the
dating circus. One man, tall and thin with black hair and a black beard,
blacker than any natural shade of hair could be. Was he a handyman? I
can see the bare shell of his work van, the tools inside, the upside-down
plastic five-gallon bucket I'd sit on while he drove, sliding around as he
turned and stopped. There was a restaurant in downtown Columbus
that he took us to. We'd never been so high up, the cityscape a view
that defied our perspective. My mother and I—now a young, bleeding
woman—in our dresses, quiet and smiling behind water glasses shaped
like our breasts. The waitstaff close at hand, replacing each sip. There
was the drive home, the long way, and a stop he had to make. Was it
his ex-wife or ex-girlfriend? He never returned to the van. My mother
knocked on a neighbor's door and called us a cab home.

If she saw him again, she never said.

———

"When she is starved, a woman will take any substitutes offered, including those that, like dead placebos, do absolutely nothing for her, as well
as destructive and life-threatening ones that hideously waste her time
and talents or expose her life to physical danger. It is a famine of the soul
that makes a woman choose things that will cause her to dance madly
out of control—then too, too near the executioner's door," Dr. Estés
continues in *Women Who Run with the Wolves*.

The other man was short and thick, white-haired and clean-shaven. While he did not look like Bob Hope, there was a kind of resemblance, perhaps an echo of that era. He drove a Jaguar and wore fitted polyester clothing. He never took us anywhere. He, instead, made out with my mother on our couch. He would stop when I crossed the room on my way to the kitchen and call out to me.

"Come over here. Let's see if you kiss like your mother."

To which my mother would throw her head back and laugh, feigning a pretend slap. "Oh stop," she'd say, and I'd disappear myself as I'd learned to do by then, as I'd watched her do to herself, to the men who consumed her, and to me.

Was the ratio of men in the dating world skewed toward the bad? Were my mother's relationships a product of this ratio, her own pattern, or a horrible fitting combination of both? Find one, throw him away, find another—always drunk on the beginning, on possibility, on the fantasy of becoming someone else.

Her pattern of disposal bore a striking resemblance to the dynamics in a country then seething with the toxicity of extreme capitalism under the Reagan administration. The myth of the American Dream was a frenzy where one could continuously dispose of one's former iteration in place of something new, new, new. Better. Dissolve roots, dismiss any connection to place and ancestry, don a mask and join the parade, wave the flag—all those stars and stripes. Perform "American" but never achieve "whiteness." In this way, my mother should have been rewarded for her level of citizenship, for her ability to embody the prescribed role.

After the disappearance of Husband Number Three, I decided I should be able to pick who my dad was, as it seemed a dad was just a man who hung around for a while, told everyone what they could and couldn't do, expected to be served and entertained, and then left. I'd begun fantasizing that my father wasn't my real father at all, and I set out to get my mother to confess to this secret. I did this when, in between courtships, she would turn to me to be her date. For brief stints, Saturday nights were reserved for the two of us at Bob Evans, where I always ordered the same thing: fried chicken, mashed potatoes, green beans, and biscuits. On the drive there and then at the table, she would hold my hand. Later, at the movie theater, I'd see groups of classmates waiting together in the ticket line, their noise and play perfectly appropriate, while my mother would smile at me and hold my hand tighter. We'd watch whatever movie wasn't sold out, our fingers interlaced. Companionship had come to be expected of me, the youngest daughter, the last daughter at home for a stretch of five years. Her emotions were mine to navigate. While she was unable to consistently care for me, I was my mother's keeper. This was the unspoken demand that imbued each moment we spent together or apart. It was expected that my devotion was for her alone.

There was another boyfriend, not long after the clowns, who appeared just after we'd moved to another town. He had a dog, a stray pup who appeared in his horse barn one day and never left. Mr. Moe. A shepherd, chow, collie mix, midsized, with perky ears and a curled tail. He was an outside dog, unless there was severe weather, and then he was permitted to lie on the screened-in porch. Worst-case scenario, he was allowed the rug just inside the front door, from which he would not stir until he was again released to the outdoors. We could never figure out where he'd come from, this patient, wise, good-natured dog, who seemed to listen with hardly a command. He stayed close to the boyfriend. They seemed to work as a team. Never sure about dogs before this, I kept my distance. Dogs had never been a part of our homes. Only cats that could be thrown away as easily as spoiled leftovers in the fridge. But Mr. Moe didn't crowd or jump, rarely barked unless he needed to protect. He was simply close—but not too close—and calm. A stroke with the tip of my shoe was as well received as a good rub of the neck and ears by the boyfriend. I settled in the presence of Mr. Moe and, soon thereafter, in the presence of the boyfriend, who grilled hamburgers for us, helped me memorize the periodic table of elements for my chemistry quizzes, and played oldies records—the Drifters, the Platters, the Everly Brothers— that we would all bop around to in the home he was building with his own two hands.

There was an engagement.

And then,

there was not.

Once it was just the two of us again, perhaps she became bored with me, or perhaps even with my presence she was lonely. I watched as she drifted in and out, unable to fully be where her body landed in any moment. The hunger to be held, adored, the attention she needed to offset her own downward spiral. She'd eventually get caught by Jesus, the only thing holding her up from a free fall into the depths of her own pain and trauma. She memorized and rehearsed scripture. Jesus was another man who could provide a temporary high. Take her away from herself, from all that she didn't want to face, and provide a fantasy—the hope that things would magically be better one day, that all suffering would end without her having to do anything differently, without anything changing, without her having to endure the chrysalis of greater awareness, self-reflective choices, and ultimately an opposing reality. I would watch her hold tightly to the word of God in between boyfriends and marriages, the forgiving heavenly father washing her clean of her sins, as she'd lie in her bed—a king-sized waterbed with mirrors in the wooden canopy above—at night, praying.

Husband Number Four snuck in after just a few months of courtship. And when my mother was done with him, or they were done with each other, not even a year had passed. He was one of the golf pros at the country club where she worked. Had it not been for my mother's employment there, I might never have seen the inside of one. The mostly older white people embedded in country club culture enjoyed visiting her small, one-chair hair salon, an amenity of privilege. An exclusive membership. Social activity available only to those of a certain class.

My mother was comforted by institutions, having been raised in them—a Catholic orphanage, the military, and then marriage. When there weren't members in need, Mami sat in her chair watching cable television, always ready to jump to attention should anyone step in wanting a trim or color. I can see her warm welcome, her laughter, putting them at ease. Perhaps a joke, which may or may not have been understood. More laughter. The customer service, the caretaking, the anticipation of a tip—our survival dependent on them.

Husband Number Four was going through a divorce. Between sessions coaching clients on their swing, he would linger in the hair salon next door to the pro shop. It was a fast-burning infatuation that led to matrimony. He was ten years younger than my mother, his daughter the same age I was when my mother divorced Husband Number One, my father. I was not kind to or playful with her. I ignored her like I did him. I could go hours, days, without talking to or looking at them.

No longer did I have the protection and strength of my two sisters. They'd moved on to their own wild, unpredictable lives some time ago. It often felt like our family of the feminine had gone from four to two down to one. Me. Alone. Our nuclear family split. My sisters with their own men now, their own patterns of dysfunction. Me hovering somewhere between childhood and womanhood with my own fantasies of what my life would be. If I had known how to grieve, I would have spent these years in a constant state of mourning. I had lost so much, and perhaps that was what I was hiding in my deep inner state, my layers of isolation.

There were the dreaded visits to Husband Number Four's parents' house, which I only vaguely recall. A condo in an upper-middle-class neighborhood. The stiff smiles. The sensation of being foreign and of trying not to touch anything—stepping carefully over the plush carpet, perching on the couch. As a teenager, I displayed a contempt for being made to join them, a vacancy I had rehearsed. This was met with cool regard, the suspicion and rejection from my "grandparents" mutual.

But there they were: the newlyweds. My mother, laughing and pretending at love. There was wine and shrimp, mussels. None of it made any sense.

What will never leave me is the image of him in my mind's eye, his spine in particular. The way his posture appeared slack, so weak it seemed as though he was going to fold completely forward, bend in on himself and slide, like a cartoon man devoid of any spine at all, onto the floor. He was a failure at standing, a poor representation of manhood. No evidence of being constructed of anything solid. But he could hit a golf ball, and he helped others with their swing, earning them golden scores. So, what did it matter that he couldn't stand up straight? And that I, at fourteen years old, noticed? Perhaps it was my own awkward, hyper-self-conscious state as an adolescent that exaggerated the look of his posture. Perhaps next to that of my military father, and other men who had passed through our family, his posture felt even more an aberration. Perhaps it was because I despised him and how privileged he was even while his whole body screamed "slacker." Or that no matter how straight my mother and I stood up or what we tried to do right, we never came close to having all that he took for granted. My ability to size up men on my mother's behalf had sharpened to a critical point. Who were these jokers she was always drunk on?

I noticed his posture more than his new Lexus sedan. The leather interior, the sunroof—my mother mistaking the car for importance. She saw possible access to his wealth, a kind of wealth that would perhaps stop the hunger/desire, which of course it didn't. The projections they created about each other as visible and fantastical as the blockbuster movies out that season: *My Girl, Beauty and the Beast, Father of the Bride.*

I rode around in the back seat silent, forced to go along with what I clearly saw as a mistake. Silence and the stink eye—the weapons of a teenager using her limited powers of presence/engagement and withholding them.

"Get that look off your face," my mother would mouth to me on any number of occasions.

All communication—verbal and nonverbal—shut down. Protests were strictly prohibited.

I felt sorry for them both. It was the first time I clearly saw my mother's addiction. This, after all, wasn't the man she was supposed to be marrying. We'd been making plans to be with another man, the boyfriend with the dog. He was still waiting for us, I knew. I had asked him to adopt me so my mother and I could have the same last name for once. Matching. My one lone identity marker fixing me to the man to whom she would say, "I do." Neat and tidy. My sisters, long gone by then, carried our father's last name until they married. I took my mother's maiden name when I turned eighteen, and I have it still.

———

Just after she'd agreed to the engagement, I confronted my mother on our blue velvet antique couch. A flea-market find, its cushions were misshapen; its springs bit into the backs of our thighs. I knew little of desire. I was a freshman in high school with two brief relationships behind me, both of which consisted of tireless tonguing and groping whenever those chaperoning turned their backs. Desire and limitations. The restriction of a zipper, parents in the front seat, braces and curfews, or the reach of a phone cord. Still, I begged her not to marry him. Told her it wouldn't work and why—his divorce was only just final, he was too young, too inexperienced to manage her, he had nothing of value to offer us, could not provide us with what we needed. In tears, she admitted she knew that everything I was saying was true. And still, she felt she had no choice.

———

"Addiction begins when a woman loses her handmade and meaningful life and becomes fixed upon retrieving anything that resembles it in any way she can. In the story, the child tries again and again to reunite with the diabolical red shoes, even though they increasingly cause her to lose control. She has lost her power of discrimination, her ability to sense what the nature of a thing really is. Because of the loss of her original vitality, she is willing to accept a deadly substitute. In analytical psychology we would say she has given the Self away," Dr. Estés clarifies.

———

There was a wedding. I must have been there, but I cannot recall a single detail. This, by now, has become my refrain. The memories that have gone missing.

Instead, I turn toward the endings. It's the endings I'm vigilant about remembering. That one moment, the men are there. They exist. And the next moment? They're gone. In a child's mind, it is due to an act of God that such things can occur, not the choices of her mother. Unless of course her mother is God, which is what I believed for a time.

The details I do remember: his pleated slacks, collared golf shirts tucked in, belt. His aviator-style eyeglasses and the excess saliva in his mouth that would pool at the edges of his thin pink lips when he spoke for too long. His laugh that met his posture—weak and apologetic. He took his place in my mother's life, his status trumping mine because he could validate her worth in a way that her daughters could not, least of all her youngest, the baby.

My mother convinced herself she could love him. She did not become any less poor, or any richer, I should say. They became more strapped for funds. We lived in cramped apartments, one in the basement of a house at the edge of a small rural town, lost in fields rowed over in crops miles and miles away from any country club. Four different addresses in one year. All in an attempt to make ends meet. I guess child support ate through nearly all his income. That and the Lexus.

At some point, we stopped going to the driving range together as a "family." No more buckets of hard, white dimpled balls. My mother's bag of clubs put somewhere out of the way.

I turned fifteen and got a learner's permit. One day instead of the Lexus, he was driving a Ford Ranger, which he used to teach me to drive. Perhaps because she worked more hours and he, for a reason I cannot recall, worked fewer. This served as a truce of sorts.

And then there were the tapes.

The tapes were copied from someone who appeared at the Friday-night gatherings we'd begun to attend at a New Age store, beyond which stood a wooded lot. The owner held regular bonfires where he told stories about Turtle Island. These were not sermons, but my mother tried them out for a time to see if they could be. At first it was a small, pedestrian group infatuated with Native American cosmology.

After a few weeks, a motlier crew started to form. Spiritual outcasts, counterculture castoffs, and outright devil worshippers began to infiltrate. But before my mother forbade our attendance, her husband was given the language tapes of a Lakota elder training the next generation of speakers. In no time, Husband Number Four was growing out his thin blond hair, had memorized all the tapes, and could talk for up to five minutes without breaking into English. What's more, he'd harvested a piece of red rock that he'd learned to make into a pipe. He'd found another Native elder who tolerated him enough to share a few things. He cut deerskin leather—bought not from a deer he'd hunted, as my mother did not offer her skills to his project—to make a simple beaded bag. He carved the stem of the pipe and used it to pray in the Lakota language. It was a masterpiece of appropriation that got him through a few months of a near midlife crisis, a real attempt à la Kevin Costner's character in *Dances with Wolves*. It was all too much for my mother.

I had already begun to starve myself by the time my mother disappeared him.

Disappearing oneself as a young woman, as a young woman of color in the face of the overculture, is not uncommon. The displays of control and of protest nothing new. But what I remember is the power of being able to dominate something essential for my survival and to do it fiercely, like any captive/prisoner—not even hunger could control me. As I could see more ribs in the mirror and the bones in my wrists and elbows and shoulders became more pronounced/sharp, I felt exhilaration. I could change shape. I wasn't trapped. What became undeniable, though I didn't have words for it at the time, was my own sovereignty as plain as the bones beneath my skin. I owned myself. I could decide if I lived or died.

———

The morning he left, never to return, Husband Number Four entered my doorless room and took a box off the top shelf of my doorless closet.

We were living in a shed we affectionately referred to as the "cabin." It had running water, when the pipes didn't freeze, and electricity. It had a washer and a dryer, albeit without proper venting. It did not have a phone. It did not receive a TV signal, but it did pick up radio signals. It lacked a real foundation, which meant that at night we could hear the nocturnal ones chewing on the wood beams that held us up. The shed was located midway up a steep hill that we had to park at the base of during winter. On the other side of the hill was an even steeper ravine. During the growing season, an abundance of black snakes slithered in the garden at the base of the hill.

He was quite stealthy. Even so, I watched him, pretending to be asleep. I watched him taking. I watched what he took. It was a box he'd given me the previous evening—the pipe he'd made and all the other materials for ceremony.

This is what lingers: his back as weak as ever, hunched and heading for the door, carrying under his arm what he'd promised me.

So silent was his absence, we did not speak of him unless one of my sisters was making a joke. Then we laughed uneasily, as if afraid of offending the spirit of the dead.

I was so convinced that he no longer existed that years later, after my own divorce, when I saw him in a health food supermarket eating with his daughter, now a young woman herself, the store tilted and spun. I had to set down my shopping basket and head for the nearest exit, to the safety and comfort of my car, where I could feel my eyes, wide and unblinking, hands trembling as if I'd seen a ghost.

I could not reckon with all the relationships, all the ruptures of my youth. I could not emotionally withstand the perpetual whiplash of disappearances, my mother's casualties. The severing from my original family of the feminine. It all forced me to evacuate moments, days, weeks, months. Evacuate myself. Spiraling deep into my imagination, into pretend, into stories.

A pattern of disappearance emerges. My own. I try tracking it.

I rarely recall the beginning of her courtships. What I can feel, what I memorize, is the breath just before the endings—all of it stacking up on itself. It has tormented me throughout my life. When all finally settles, when life quiets and perhaps even love curls up, I brace myself against the fear, the terror of a sudden disappearance—of those I've come to love, and/or myself. Taken away. Suddenly gone from me forever.

Perhaps it was exhaustion that finally released my mother. Perhaps her parallel to the little girl in the story's feet being cut off—to rid her for good of the red shoes and their terrible dancing—was her return to the boyfriend with the dog, resuming their engagement and then marrying him. Husband Number Five, the last. The one who lasted. And perhaps because he had grown up working with horses on a farm on the Ohio/Indiana state line, had experience with mental instability with his first wife, and was a high school history teacher who mentored poor, disadvantaged inner-city youth, he knew how to be steady. He knew cycles, knew how to show up, knew how not to get thrown by an animal spooked by what wasn't there. I guess he won her. He had patiently waited out Husband Number Four. After my mother broke off their engagement, he had hoped for her return. Written her letters, which she never shared with me. The two of them picked up where they'd left off.

While I don't remember that wedding either, I do remember it was on New Year's Eve, their vows coinciding with making resolutions and shedding the old, welcoming in the new. A small gathering at his house afterward. The relief I felt, and I imagine my sisters did, too, that the dancing was coming to an end. Fifteen years of possessed dancing, which I'd endured from ages three to nearly eighteen, which had taken so much from me—including my own mother.

I'll never know how and why the commitment of matrimony finally took. Why the promises finally meant something. My own departure from home was imminent. I myself was poised to leap into my own wild, unpredictable life just as my sisters had before me. There would've been no one to hold my mother's hand, to tether her, to emotionally nurse her. Perhaps this influenced her ability to stick it out. In the face of her last child leaving—another form of abandonment that pulsed in her original wounding—her ability to commit was strengthened. Or perhaps it was truly love. She had finally found, and returned to, her right match.

My mother remains a riddle to me. Incomprehensible. Her abilities, her inabilities. What she has been able to survive—from institutions, from husbands, from others, from herself. The never-ending gesture—physical or energetic—of getting back up, never ceasing to find the energy to try again, which she has owned in this life.

I could not have saved her, saved us, from the repetition of her choices, the consequences of harm. For so long, I believed otherwise. I worked for years to bend into a shape that would support her weight, my trunk contorted in a twist of uncanny strength, my roots feeling the constant force of being pulled up by the significance of her perpetual need while I willed them to reach farther and farther down—and eventually away from her.

———

Later in her life, after celebrating wedding anniversaries with Husband Number Five for nearly thirty years, my mother is adamant about disappearing the decades of her former self. It is in the past. She has been forgiven by God. Quick to change the subject, to cry foul, rejecting any reflection, processing, or detailing of that time; what was difficult, what pained, what was learned, what we now know to be true, how we were changed, would be forever changed, is not spoken of, is not even tolerated.

Expected in the forgiveness I have given her is my silence. She has her excuse—her own terrible childhood—which trumps any grievance her daughters could nurse about her or their early lives. My young life, all the years I'd known up to age seventeen in our home, no longer mine to discuss, to cite, to claim—for better or worse. My memories and the stories I create to make sense of those years and to conjure some kind of healing, she perceives as a betrayal. Another way I choose myself over her. The grieving inherent in such a serious ultimatum continues in our estrangement, a constant echoing of loss.

*"One of the most fundamental principles of Somatic Archaeology [is]
that healing comes as a direct result of empowered action,
of recognizing our choices, and of making change.
Again, we heal and we remember when we feel safe enough to do so.
Empowerment is safety."*

—RUBY GIBSON, *MY BODY, MY EARTH*

CHANGING SHAPE,

PART I

1

I HOLD THE MEMORY CLOSE AS IF IT WERE THIS:

The curtains twirled and spun with the breeze. In my mother's bedroom, darkness. Everything appeared falsely clean and glowed white—the walls, the sheets, our teeth. I was the skin on my mother's skin. Eldest Sister's and Older Sister's limbs woven together. All of us twined like netting across my mother's bed.

I couldn't sleep. I was hungry.

I must have been four or five. My sisters must have been twelve and thirteen. And our father must have been with another Spanish-speaking woman—Mexican, but what was the difference to him—who was already fattening with another life.

In my mother's bed, in her arms, our skin seamless. She was my sustenance.

Perhaps she hoped for a miracle, ignoring what her body couldn't do. Thinking that once again she could feed me, give me what I needed as she had when I was an infant. She offered her breast even though there was no longer milk.

I was the baby.

I am told I will always be the baby.

I hung on to my mother, her large brown nipple in my mouth, and it calmed me. No milk and still the hunger, but the body of my mother, closer.

2

The first massages I gave were to my mother. Her feet ached after standing on them for nine, ten, twelve hours a day in shoes too flimsy for such a task. Once my sisters left home at seventeen and eighteen years of age, I was the only one who could offer my mother and her feet any relief. The palms of my eleven-year-old hands traced her heels, worked the skin between her toes, dug into her arches. No matter what cream I used, layers of dead skin always remained on one foot, curled and hardened, brittle yet stubbornly attached, as if my mother had once been a sea creature covered with scales and had turned human, and all of her body had obeyed except this one foot, which, when fully dry, felt like it was coated in wood shavings.

When I was too tired to knead her feet, or just didn't feel like it, she'd plead with me to "pick at" her foot, as if that took less energy. A decade later, after studying massage therapy—Swedish techniques at first—I practiced on my mother. The long, slow glides of effleurage, the kneading movements of petrissage: lighter at the tendons and ligaments, firmer at the belly of muscles. I massaged her neck, and her limbs, hips, stomach, and back. My thumbs pulling the skin in small circles away from her spine. My palms pushing the blood toward her heart.

3

No matter my personal journey, no matter the torment of her chaos, my mother remains my home well into my thirties. Here, with her, is where all begins and ends. "I gave you life," she often reminded me when I tried to defy her as a preteen, then a teenager, attempts at individuation steeped in attitude. "I can take it away." It was used as a threat or a joke, depending on the circumstance in which we squared off.

The compact, sturdy build of her—her petite frame, caramel-colored skin, brown eyes, coarse, tightly coiled dark hair—ordinary among so many other Puerto Rican women, so many Caribbean women.

And her swimmer's shoulders, made as if she were ocean bound.

My shoulders the same.

I cannot swim like her. She forgets that she didn't teach me, that it's a skill that must be learned. No matter how many times I've been taught as an adult, just like with the Spanish language, I can never remember how to do it correctly.

I'd like to think that I could save my own life if I were unable to touch the bottom, that I'd be able to tread water or float on my back, where I could then fling my arms over, back, and around to propel me to some place unseen, the backstroke—or perhaps something that resembles it—keeping me above water for a limited period of time. But the weight of me always threatens to sink. My lungs have always felt weak. I prefer to touch some kind of ground. Head exposed so I can safely breathe.

Our bodies give us away, chart our emotions with physical manifestations. In Chinese medicine, the lungs represent grief. Any condition that includes the lungs cannot be separated from an underlying relationship with grief, conscious or unconscious. In depth psychology and Jungian dream analysis, water often symbolizes our emotions. Beneath the appearances we cultivate, the personalities we perform, there are our emotional bodies with their endless nautical miles, no land in sight, and for many of us, the weight of our grief-stricken lungs threatening to drown us.

4

It's my mother's smell I can still summon:

Jōvan musk oil from the drugstore. It permeated the dollar bill pulled from the inside of her bra she would give me as I headed into preschool. I would conjure her all day as I smelled it. A thick penetrating scent of low notes reminiscent of pine needles, indistinct animal sweetness, or bark in a state of decay on the forest floor, perhaps green roses shedding their petals, or a bouquet of white flowers with long throats just about to bloom; shadow and sunlight. And for under ten dollars a bottle at the time she purchased it, none of these things. She rolled the applicator across her neck and chest, leaving a thin line that glistened. Next, she'd dust her skin with Johnson & Johnson baby powder, a trail of white that continued down her torso and beyond the waistband of her nylon underwear. She used Johnson & Johnson, for the all-American baby, on herself and on me. I remember being spread out on the living room floor at four years old, supine on a towel after a bath, as she applied the powder and massaged my limbs, wrung out my arms and legs, made circles on my chest and stomach. As I lay naked on the floor, all my limbs relaxed and extended. In my memory, I'm peering down at myself from the ceiling, a starfish, five-pointed including my neck and head. Held in place by my mother's love and attention. Anointed. No fear at all about being exposed and carried away by the deep current of indescribable, overwhelming emotion.

5

Not until my thirties would I consider unfolding the map of my mother so that it included her parents and their parents, my aunts and uncles in other areas of the country—rare visits and occasional phone calls—as unfamiliar but relevant coordinates, that I would try to see her in relation to them, as on a continuum of ancestral life, an extension of a family of siblings that tried to reorganize themselves after the youngest three emerged from the Catholic orphanage where they'd been deposited.

After all, to locate my mother was to locate myself. In order to embark on a journey into new territory, one must first understand where they are. To whom and what they've belonged.

Before this understanding, it was only my mother that mattered. My world began and ended within the bounds of her body. The force she used when willing herself to show up for work—hours on her feet, her hands lifted above her shoulders, the scissors and comb extensions of her fingers—no matter if fatigue struck her or she didn't feel well. If her body faltered, if her body fell ill, what would happen to us, to me? Wouldn't my body also cease, my existence unravel? She was the whole of my world, as a mother is for her child, but while other children's lives expanded from the safety of their homes, mine was defined by uncertainty. The limits that defined my reality followed the outline of her body, the expanse of her breath, and her stories—about herself and about the world, with mental, emotional, energetic, spiritual subtexts—defining what could and could not be. I did not question her. I absorbed it all. I pledged myself to her.

Her emotional upsets were our only constant, her continuous grief and heartache, the anxiety that threatened to whisk her away into a whirl of activity, or the depression that transformed her, threatened to submerge her into a never-ending slumber. I soothed and steadied her with my presence.

No matter what direction my life took, there was a felt expectation that I would never leave her or put anyone or anything above her. Other women who might be mother figures were cut out of my life as quickly as they showed themselves. Throughout my preteen and teenage years, if I challenged her or upset her with my tone of voice, with an expression on my face she found defiant, she would strike without warning. A slap, a flurry of slaps across my face and my head, until she was exhausted by her own effort. Only then would she leave me to make sense of what'd happened. Rearranging my hair ties that had come loose, wiping at my face slick with hot tears, anger clenching my throat, the burn of shame on my skin for deserving to be treated in such a way. My eyes unblinking at the shock and humiliation of such a betrayal. That her loving hands could and would deliver pain. The one I devoted myself to saw me worthy of such punishment, disgrace. The force coming at my head from a person I would've trusted to protect me from such a blow.

I learned to watch her as if watching a weathervane for wind direction. Did she sing church songs as we walked from our apartment to the parking lot? Did she say, "Praise God," when her car started, when the rain held off long enough to leave her hair undisturbed and her efforts to straighten it intact, when a customer left her a generous tip? Or was she silent, with not even a threat of shadow on her face? Did she remind me how fleeting life was, how she could be taken at any time, how our only guarantee of staying together would be in heaven? Did she make jokes about the lack of food or not being able to pay rent? What would we do then? I wanted to know. Where would we go? As if knowing would make it manageable.

"Cardboard box on the street corner," she'd say, exasperated.

I never knew whether to believe her.

Hearing this at eleven or twelve or thirteen or fourteen, without my older sisters to buffer me, fractured any sense of trust. No matter how fine things appeared, despite any momentary comfort of familiarity, calmness and security, chaos and destruction, separation and abandonment loomed. This was her childhood imprint overlaid onto mine. Without close study, they could be the same, her story and mine. My experience, her experience. Her emotions, my emotions.

6

Perhaps this is how it went:

"It's not enough"—the lock in the doorknob copper-colored, horizontal, and half sunk like a penny in a candy machine coin slot—"to keep somebody from trying to come in and get you." There are all kinds of monsters in the night. It's Satan's fault. We stand facing the incompetent back door.

I lean my head against the small of her back.

"Are you watching?" she wants to know.

My mother repeatedly instilled a fear in me that I could be taken, stolen away any moment we were not together. I was suspicious of strangers. I kept a safe distance from those I somewhat knew but not well enough. Any motion toward me, the sensation of someone following me, an unexplained sound nearby or in our home—whichever one we could afford at the time—was immediately worrisome; a man, woman, or teenager looking at me longer than what was socially acceptable put me on edge. I learned to be vigilant.

———

At a local strip mall, in the back of a discount coat store, McGruff the Crime Dog stood among folks wearing TAKE A BITE OUT OF CRIME T-shirts. They made a photo ID for me and asked for any distinguishing features that would possibly identify me if needed. At eight years old, I told them about the black mole near my belly button. I was given a short talk on safety, none of which I heard, as I tried not to imagine my stomach separated from the rest of me in a ditch or a cornfield, the black mole my name tag. Seeing children on milk cartons was a daily reality; after-school specials on network TV reinforced the concern about kidnappings and killings. Vans were notorious vehicles of crime. Later, as an adult, I would wonder: How serious was the threat? Who would have wanted a little mixed-race, brown-skinned girl in rural Ohio in the 1980s? Who besides my own family would have cared if I had gone missing? Was my mom's concern about the possibility of my being abducted more a reflection of her own terror, her childhood trauma of being left at a Catholic orphanage? Or was it deeper than that, a pulsing shrill in her island girl's unconscious of Indigenous and African enslaved women as their children were stolen? Was it what most mothers of color struggled with every day as they fought to provide for their families while institutions created to keep safe, serve, and support stole the humanity and innocence of their children, their daughters?

But on this night, on these nights, a man is waiting. Her date. It always seems a gamble—will he be the kind of man who provides and protects or the kind of man who takes and harms? She is blinded by the thought of winning. Her patent leather high heels strike the floor. Gum snaps in her back teeth. It all sounds like dance music.

"Pay attention," she says, dragging a chair from the kitchen table and lodging it beneath the doorknob. "This is how you protect yourself. I want you to be safe." Her lips are warm and tacky with lipstick. She marks my face.

My sentry, the wooden chair taken from the kitchen table, propped unnaturally, for my sake, onto its two back legs against the door.

She'll be back "soon," which is of course a relative term, but she instructs me not to worry. My sisters have found parties to attend. I park myself in front of the TV with a can of Pringles and watch a string of shows—*Family Ties, Webster, The Cosby Show, Cheers, Magnum P.I., Night Court,* and whatever else comes in clear—well into the night while I wait for someone to return.

7

The rooms were small, just large enough for the massage table, a chair, a stand for the clock/CD player, and a dimmed floor lamp towering in one of the corners. A stool where I'd sit while working on a client's neck and head tucked out of the way. If there was a window, the blinds were pinched closed. Perhaps a hook or two on the back of the door, sometimes a mirror no larger than the viewer's head, also hidden behind an open door. A poster of the human body—a "universal" white male— layers of tissues stripped off half of him to reveal fasciae, muscles, veins/ arteries, bones. A file for each client, pages of intake forms and SOAP (Subjective, Objective, Assessment, and Plan) charts, a necessity for the clinic—as the charts tracked progress—and for health insurance pur- poses, as many clients had a prescription for the massage therapy they received. On the table, layers of blankets, a heating pad, a fitted or flat sheet tied tightly at both ends, a bolster for beneath their knees when they were looking at the ceiling, beneath their ankles when they were looking at the floor.

The client sat in the chair and listened to me explain how I would touch them, address their pain, the problems their bodies presented. "I'll check in with you," I'd say, "about whether the pressure is too much or not enough. If you're ever uncomfortable for any reason, please let me know." I would instruct the client to lie on their back, between the sheets, beneath the blanket, and position their knees over the bolster for support. They were instructed to remove all clothing down to their underwear or to remove that as well if they were comfortable doing so. The music alone seemed to induce audible sighs of relaxation. I would step out, giving them their privacy, running my cold hands under warm water after washing them.

We hold memories in our tissues, and it can be surprising how we respond—sudden laughter or tears, unbearable pain that can make us clench—to only the suggestion of being touched. Sliding my left hand beneath the bottom sheet to rest on someone's lower back, my right hand gently positioned over the blanket on top of their stomach, and breathing with them for several minutes could be enough to melt away a pattern of holding, a knot in the stomach. Beneath the veneer of muscle tension, strains, spasms, and chronic pain—a sort of protection—perhaps, was anger they couldn't admit to and had to swallow or a deep dissatisfaction, a hunger that went unnamed. No matter the details, which only they knew, I moved slowly, with their permission, following their body's lead.

After quietly reentering the room, I would check the lighting, check their temperature—offering a heating pad or hot towels if needed—check the music, which was audible but easy to ignore. Was it still relaxing to them? Once they were comfortable, I'd slip my shoes off and slide them under the table.

Holding the client's hand, I'd ground myself through my feet, breathing through the energy moving through my soles, expanding and opening my chest and upper back, relaxing my belly, softening my gaze, watching the client in the periphery of my vision. I'd wait to feel their breath as it descended into the palm of their hand. I gathered useful information in those first few moments. Did they hold out their rigid arm, their hand pressed unnaturally stiff, or did it go slack as they surrendered it for me to hold, relax into a curl of loose fist? Where was the tension? What was the quality of the tension? Did they hold their breath, breathe only with their upper chest, or did the breath travel freely into the low belly and lower back with each inhalation? I needed to know how much they were willing to receive so I could gauge how best to meet them. Their willingness to let go or awareness of their own restrictions and patterns dictated whether they would resist or assist me in unwinding and releasing the stress metabolizing in their physical form. Just because they sought help didn't mean they would accept it. It was less about categorizing and judging them and more about discerning what was best when providing their therapy.

I slowly guided their wrist back and forth in a snaking motion, releasing tension in the joint, gathering more information. Noticing. The sigh. The fluttering of closed eyelids. The silence or incessant talking. The gurgling in the stomach, often a sign of a deeper state of relaxation. The stillness or shifting. And beyond that, what the words beneath the words communicated. The presence beneath the silence. The quality of energy. The willingness or resistance. Subtleties. Each body sharing its story.

8

"Mini-me," my mother would say, as if I'd been cast from her, my life's sole purpose to replicate her. Any headache, any fever, any stomach upset of hers, I felt, too, as if it were my own. It comforted us and affirmed that we were the same—that I was an extension of her. My sense of belonging was clear and definite. I was hers. To be included was to be owned. How could she ever see that this resembled island–U.S. relations? The subtext of propaganda infusing what she thought was just the way things were. Ownership means you've been saved, means you'll survive, means you've been claimed, means you have a place. But in the case of island–U.S. relations, the belonging is more decoration than substance, more gesture than inclusion. Love equaled being controlled and trying to control, a manipulating force.

She was mine, too, at least in the moments she was free from the flock of circling men, their interest as unceasing as buzzards' wings. Her delight in their acknowledgment, her need for their flickering attention, her dependency on courtship and fantasy a threat to what we shared. Men were mythical beings, monsters, ready to threaten with their inherent need to dominate. She created a dependency on them while issuing a warning that one of them would come to take me away.

Beware. Stay on guard.

I held my mother's hands. I held my mother's feet. I held my mother, my focal point, my compass, all the directions and coordinates she contained.

———

In my forties, I will turn to Toko-pa Turner's *Belonging*. As a professor in an MFA Interdisciplinary Arts program at Goddard College, I suggest it to my students, beneath whose creative practices lies a persistent need to locate and experience their own belonging. As it turns out, the advice I give to my students, I will be most in need of myself. This section of the book will transcend all my coping and defense mechanisms.

> The Death Mother is a term for this energy or archetype that resents, abandons, and even wants to destroy her child. . . . As the Death Mother's target, the child eventually develops the conviction that she is living in a dangerous world and that her life is at risk. But long after leaving the family home, the child is haunted by the Death Mother, who campaigns against her from the inside out.

Reading these words was a moment of brutal reckoning. My mother's reach went only so far, but I had extended her reach, continued her behavior in how I related to myself when she was across the country going about her own daily life. If I didn't belong just to my mother and her wounding, if I didn't belong just to our family and our trauma, where else, to whom else, did I belong?

9

In between clients, and on breaks throughout my workday, I closed the door and opened the window. Sunlight permeating. The massage table became a makeshift desk. I pulled books from my oversized purse and fanned them across the table, turning the clock face so I could time my freewriting. I submitted to my hand as it liberated me in my notebook—a place for all my new and awkward truth telling. Notebooks amassed. My voice cut through and surprised me. I was not pretending, I was confronting. My pen pulled me away from my incessant drive to please others, provided temporary relief when on the page. I clung to the concrete, sensory details present moment by moment. Something holy emanates from all things ordinary. A fleck of dirt on the plush crimson rug in the shape of a fingernail; a hushed conversation in the hall—the words *diagnosis* and *protocol;* earlier, on my way to the massage clinic, giant sycamores whiter than bone along the river.

When I finish writing and return to my relationships and my life, I must traverse the vast space that separates how I present myself and conduct my life from the ceremonial quality of being submerged in my writing, surpassing my superficial performances.

This will be the way it is for quite some time.

Years later, when I assemble my writing into stories of truth and fiction and begin publishing them, my extended family—my mother's siblings—attacks, my aunt writing a letter to an editor disowning me. I retreat from what I share. My attempt to honor was violently returned to me, rejected. I shut myself away. Hiding how I crumble, how thoroughly I've been shaken. As my voice is stifled by the threat of others—primarily the aunt who leads the charge—I turn to the code of metaphor, to the language of the mythic.

I know better than to surrender my voice to her. I cannot escape the fact that it was our ancestors, hers and mine, whose tongues were cut out, faces branded. Our bodies that remember the tortures of betraying the master. As a woman, I know the imbalance and sickness of turning away from the inner experience of ourselves, the self-inflicted harm of denying ourselves our own truth.

But even as she demands that I behave, I will not turn her into what I've come to fear—the perpetrator lurking at every turn, ready to strip me of my ability to define, assert, claim, and protect myself. I will not construct a story in which I am the victim. I will not let it be that simple.

10

Under threat of persecution, disappearance, and murder, twentieth-century Latin American writers—mainly Isabel Allende, Jorge Luis Borges, Eduardo Galeano, Pablo Neruda, and Gabriel García Márquez—turned their writing into code. On the page, they employed symbols that spoke like dreams. They tilted reality so that it slid into the realm of the surreal. Relied on images and symbols to hold the intrinsic structure of a piece. Because of this, they could continue writing and publishing, an adaptation for survival that I understood and adopted. Reality became magical; the natural became supernatural. Real. Not real. Hyper-real.

My understanding of these authors and their works is constantly changing and evolving. I've become less interested in the othering term "magical realism" that defines this way of writing, positioning it as somehow less grounded than its counterpart of realism. The ever-involved process of becoming, seeing, and knowing can never, should never, be limited by what is real or not real as defined by those in positions of power. I see this in writing workshops when perspectives and experiences differ. A white student might tell a Native and/or Black student that some moment or detail in their story could never happen. Unchecked conditioning and limited thinking undermine a person's ability to express what is personally "real" for them. If I were pressed to choose a name for these seminal writings, I would call them liminal fiction. Work that denotes the subconscious and the unseen as necessary and valuable counterparts to the conscious and seen.

Nothing about history and humans is as simple as the reductions we attempt to make. Indigenous and African futurism that contains "magical realism" and "science fiction" does so not only to escape harmful, oppressive histories and realities but also to align with and reclaim cultural cosmologies, celebrating a knowing in opposition to dominant, mainstream society and its ongoing forces of colonization. The focus is not with the individual, in isolation, as the source of strength, but with the collective, with communities empowered. Not the universe, but the multiverse. No longer is the single voice reliable or even desirable but rather a polyphony of perspectives. All is relational. Where we point the attention of our pen—to characters, to places, to the details of a world seen and unseen but also stubbornly existing—is also pointing its attention back at us. It is a relational stance.

My liminal stories look like this:

When a girl becomes a woman, she is no longer permitted the use of her legs. She must find another way to transport herself.

If her father loves her, he will construct a cart. It will be wide enough for her hips and narrow enough for her to pass others with ease as she slips down sidewalks. Negotiating intersections—clogged with the legs of men, bicycles, motorbikes, buses, taxis, and trucks—with grace depends on the quality of her father's craftsmanship.

If her mother loves her, she will help her daughter paint her cart. A design to call attention, bright colors of lime, tangerine, and lemon. This will help reduce the risk of being unseen. Mothers have also been known to sew their daughters rabbit-skin gloves, the only barrier against the chafe of spinning wheels.

To protect her from the constant ache of the sun, an umbrella is fixed above her. This provides a small circumference of shade.

It is the younger women, strong and stubborn, who propel themselves beyond the walls of their family compound. Middle-aged women and elderly women are content to collapse inside the home with their slop of legs hidden by elaborately embroidered blankets.

Cooking, eating, cleaning, visiting, and sleeping all take place on the floor. The ground is the woman's place. From here, she gazes up at the men, watches the moving legs of her children.

If a husband loves his wife, he will carry her. Not so often as to spoil her, but on rare, unexpected occasions. This will keep her alternately hopeful and disappointed.

When a woman is married, she is no longer permitted to speak. She may clap when she needs to demonstrate a matter of great importance. All other communication happens with hand gestures, her fingers wild insects hooking and flicking the air.

When a woman is pregnant with her first child, if she is loved by her sisters, she is given her own personal knife. A blade to hide under the wrap of her shawl, sharp enough to cut.

Every month, the girl children of each family are brought into the largest room of the house and asked to sing the traditional songs, asked to trot and canter. The men and boys stand against the walls mesmerized by the whirling pairs of limbs, the mess of quick feet. The men and boys narrow their eyes. Pull at the skin or hair on their chins. Smile and shake their heads.

In the hall, the women of the house listen to the girls' voices, feel the locomotion of their legs pounding the planks of the floor. The vibration travels beneath the elaborately embroidered blankets, through the skin and blood. It agitates the muscles, scrambles the nerves. The women grab at their shawls, try to shield themselves from the memory, but still, deep inside them, it pricks and crawls.

———

When I read stories steeped in metaphor in front of an audience, I nearly weep. People seem traumatized, feeling the emotional current beneath the language. How strange was I to have written such things? Again, I think of the authors who survived under regimes the surveillance of which tugged at their pens, pressed a choke hold against their voice. The greater the threat, it seems, the more stunning the supernatural in their writing. Speaking beyond the mental confines of what can and what cannot be, the internal communicated the eternal. What can only be felt. Traps set for cosmologies thousands of years old. Language becomes winged, startles off the page.

11

Sleep was the one place we could afford to go, dreams an accessible destination. Growing up, when I didn't feel well, I would retreat into my bedroom and shut the door, hide beneath the covers nearly unresponsive. For days. I was often sick—perhaps it was stress, my lack of nutrition, a virus, another fever, another migraine, menstrual cramps. Or the overwhelm of too much stimulation, the onslaught to my nervous system like trying to touch the bottom as water filled my nose. The voices of kids at school, their shouts and screams, their piercing laughter; the constant buzzing of fluorescent lights; rows of incomprehensible algebra on the chalkboard. The thick stench of coffee and nicotine on Mrs. Greyson's breath as she kneeled down to assist me with X and Y equations; thawing worms and frogs waiting to be dissected; the pungent cologne of the man in my mother's life, the clash of it with her own perfume as they attempted a mating dance; my mother's voice breathing into our answering machine, recording a message that greeted callers, any caller, like foreplay—a friend who hears it reports to others that my mother sounds like a phone sex worker. All of it, I felt; emotions turned into physical assaults.

The secretary would call my mother. I'd wait until she had a break in hair appointments for her to pull up to the school's front doors.

Her quiet was difficult to read. She could've been upset that my sickness was disrupting her schedule, that the money she'd spend when stopping at the grocery store on the way home to buy the same things she always did to remedy me—NyQuil, Sprite, saltine crackers, cans of Campbell's chicken noodle soup, or Advil and packages of generic ramen—was money we desperately needed to pay bills. Was she distant because of me or because of another problem worrying her? My mother would drop me off at home and drive back to work. I would gather the grocery sack and my bookbag and head into our rental alone. If I could manage heating up the soup, I would. If not, I'd take a sleeve of crackers and a glass of Sprite, place them next to my bed, and drink a dose of NyQuil. My mother's intermittent and unpredictable love and care, her lack of consistent responsibility as the adult in charge, and her cycles of neglect created in me a vigilance and desperate need to track what was far beyond my comprehension. Once my sisters fledged and went out into the world, there was more often than not no one to take care of me. It was not uncommon for my mother to spend nights away from me—at parties, with dates—where I was unable to reach her. At twelve, thirteen, and fourteen years old, I would fix myself Hamburger Helper and wait at my post on the couch for morning, when it was safe for me to close my eyes and rest, finally, as if the sun and its light would protect me.

When my mother was sick, I would comfort her, worry over her. She received my full attention, my concern. This was our unspoken agreement. When I was unwell, it was better for me not to bother her and to figure out how to fix myself, so as not to overwhelm her. A woman of color, a single mother, in rural Ohio, down on luck, love, and money most of the time. Sunday mornings she sat in some church pew, surrounded by white couples and white families with their stability and their security and their steady incomes, as if that would save us. As if being near them would transpose their reality onto us. And maybe in some ways it did, got us to the next day. She had to be well to be any version of a mother, and her being well enough was my responsibility. That, and the ongoing ability to feel what she felt.

12

It wasn't long into my career as a massage therapist that I began studying other modalities and techniques: in therapeutic touch, craniosacral therapy, lymphatic drainage techniques, trigger point therapy, Reiki, reflexology, aromatherapy, prenatal massage, hot stone massage, and elements of Shiatsu and Thai massage. All informed how I responded to a client's needs. Simultaneously, I came to realize how much time I spent nowhere near my body in order to tolerate moments of insecurity, uncomfortable emotions, or isolation. My body felt like the thing that I was constantly escaping.

During countless workshops over the fifteen years that I worked in the healing arts, it became customary for me to receive bodywork—experiencing what I offered my clients, and learning through conversations with other practitioners, some of them elders in the field, about all the many ways to support wellness. Herbs, plants, food, tinctures, homeopathic remedies, meditation, exercise. The mind-body connection was explicit and prioritized.

The more time I spent learning to occupy my own body and trust the sensations and information it provided me, the more physical, mental, and emotional self-awareness I developed. I trusted this awareness. I trusted myself. What did I feel physically? What did I notice and understand? How did I make meaning, create a story, in the face of the input this new awareness afforded me? How did the stories I created make me feel emotionally? How did they alter the physical sensations I had, my mental capacity, the understandings I had?

At a certain point, I switched to seeing my chronic pain as an instructor. What was it my body was asking me to turn my compassionate attention toward? My chronic neck pain, a result of whiplash I'd suffered in car accidents, also came to symbolize the tendency to look back, gaze fixed on the past, as if distrustful of what might be approaching from behind. If my neck burned, it was time to slow down or stop. I needed to turn away from others and redirect my care toward myself. I employed what I'd come to know as tools of relief, like stretching and magnesium, fish oil, arnica, and other anti-inflammatory supplements, in addition to affirmations. *I do not rely on my past to define me. I am safe to reimagine my life and focus on what is here and now. I can trust what I cannot see, what lies ahead.* My chronic neck pain has diminished significantly over the years with this kind of care. When it resurfaces, I don't feel like I've done something wrong and am being punished. I don't attack myself. I quietly notice and give myself good care. I slow down, find a way to rest a little more, to take full breaths that soften my posture. I drink more water. I'm honest with myself about what self-care can resolve and what it cannot, like systematic racism and oppression. And eventually, I come out the other end affirmed by showing up for myself, knowing that I'm worthy of my own attention and compassion. I don't ignore or dismiss how I feel. I don't pretend away pain; I meet it and move with it until it eventually subsides.

I began to discern my experiences, to see when these had been over-taken by others. When I was feeling their sensations of pain and discomfort, of fear and embarrassment, of restriction and sadness, as my own. I had always rushed to fulfill others' needs, prioritizing them over mine as I had with my mother. This awareness happened slowly, in layers and over time. Initially only with clients.

I learned to sense sexual undertones or a client's unspoken intention and would quickly secure draping, redirect a hand on the verge of wandering to my lower back or leg as I passed by the table, or turn my head away as I felt the charge, the heat and electricity they were directing at me, when I was leaning into their back using my forearms or elbows for greater pressure, my face and chest inches from their skin. If needed, I would speak to the moment, calling out any lurking behavior that threatened my safety. Some people confused the caring touch that they did not receive from anyone else—not even from a lover or spouse—and attention to their body as sexual. In such cases, I would have to correct them and explain that my interest was in their health, and that it was professional, that I adhered to ethical standards. If this didn't clear things up—and on a few occasions, it did not—I would end the massage, directing the client to get dressed, and I'd leave the room. Security or front desk staff would be waiting to escort the client off the premises. The other confusion was with clients expecting to be rescued or spontaneously fixed, or who gave orders as if I were another of their employees—personal assistant, nanny, housekeeper, gardener—another number, not a person, whose entire life was in service to theirs.

The necessary boundaries imposed in the massage room and the controlled proximity to others' bodies made me more attuned to my own body. I came to fully occupy my physical body and trust what I felt and intuited, learned how to differentiate between myself and another, and developed an unwavering confidence in protecting my boundaries, both personal and professional.

I ignored the comments by other massage therapists about the "dirty" white sheets after working on Black clients. Their accumulation of skin cells sloughing off just like white clients' but visible because of the pigmentation. Instead, I focused on my clients. The body lying before me on the table. Vulnerable, belly up, unclothed, and swaddled in blankets.

Most of my clients were body-weary folks desperate for relief and to feel at home in their own skin, to access their own capacity to be well—men who dragged themselves through long hours working at a desk, endured weeks of grueling labor, or commuted to and from jobs that robbed them of themselves; women contorted by contraptions that made them "attractive," exhausted and riddled with pain they had forgotten to feel; pregnant women whose babies rolled and kicked in their bellies as I massaged the mamas' legs and hands; adolescents coping with the tenderness, extreme self-consciousness, and crippling vulnerability of being caught shedding their childhood while their adulthood skin hadn't yet fully grown in; couples with their spoken and silent exchanges, loving rapport, threats, or domination palpable in the air around us. Occasionally, they weren't body weary at all, but children who could either barely lay still, who farted and laughed, or who instantly fell into a deep, healing sleep.

I transitioned from clinical to spa settings. The clientele transformed into the wealthy and sometimes the famous. In addition to my shifts at the spa, I would also make house calls—which represented a significant increase in pay but required me to haul the table and bags of sheets, towels, blankets, and bolsters for an experience worth the price.

If a client complained of chronic headaches, neck pain, or stomach issues, I would place my hands gently on the area and listen. My ability to relieve discomfort and restore a sense of health and well-being—a felt improvement, often significant—increased as I touched more bodies. Emotional distress disguised as physical pain, calmed by guiding clients through breathwork and passive stretches in which I pushed and pulled joints beyond what they could typically do. A body on the table sunk into a state of rest and repair that evaded them elsewhere.

Thousands of bodies, a decade and a half, countless stories, the ability of a pair of hands—mine—aligned in an ancient practice of healing through touching, allowing the body to lead in its own health and healing. Unlike with my mother, I learned that through boundaries, with self-compassion, and by including myself and advocating for my own needs, I was able to provide care that didn't eclipse and exhaust me. The laying on of hands. Mine not always but nearly always the darker set.

13

I imagine the ingredients: flour, water, lard.

"This is how you feed your family, comadre—it's cheap, and it lasts. Watch my hands."

On the military base then known as Fort Hood, while husbands and fathers marched the streets in their units, cleaned guns, and smoked outside the PX, my Puerto Rican mother and her Mexican neighbor patted out one tortilla after another. The clapping of their hands music for the hungry.

Two years later, with my mother newly divorced, the food changes. We divide scraps from places where we never step foot. What we put into our mouths are not whole foods that we prepare and cook ourselves but instant, processed foods in boxes and pouches dropped into boiling water or microwaved. There is little time to make tortillas. Their appearance is rare. We exist in a chaos that sends my mother back to a regressed state. She is not a parent of three in her early thirties; she is another girl alongside her daughters, struggling to behave as an adult.

Our hunger remains, remembers.

I hold the memory close as if it were this:

In our duplex, Mami spills out her leftovers. She's just returned from a date with a man who refused to let her bring us along, or perhaps she knew better than to ask. Cold stuffed clams, chicken Parmesan, shrimp scampi smack loudly as they all hit the plate. At midnight, in the middle of her bed, we jab our small forks into the dwindling pile of food. She adds water to stretch generic milk, pours it over Raisin Bran, and crunches while we fill our cheeks with food we don't know how to pronounce.

———

Perhaps this is how it went:

In my mother's powder-blue two-door Ford complete with eight-track player, I sit in the front seat, crowding her. Hungry and whining. At four years old, I could not be soothed by anything she said. I could not eat her words.

Finally, she says, "I've got just the thing."

I unstick my bare skin from the vinyl, draw my knees underneath me, and wait for her—my single mother, the magician—to make appear, out of thin air, something to eat. She raises her bare arm in front of my mouth. My loose hair whips about, the wind from the open windows teasing it into knots.

"Here," she says. "Eat."

We had just left the house she cleaned. With this money, she paid her way through barber school. Lorain was the biggest city we would ever inhabit, before we began trading one small rural Ohio town for another. The house was owned by a Japanese doctor and his wife. He was always working, while his wife, in full designer dress—polyester slacks, printed blouse, jewelry, makeup, and modest heels—followed me around, as I followed my mother around. We were a house parade. My mother led, a folded bandana fastened around her head, a can of Ajax and a bottle of Pine-Sol rattling in the empty bucket she carried along with a mop.

If my mother had pride, she certainly didn't bring it into the doctor's house with her. On all fours, she shined the parquet flooring, soles turned up as she dragged her knees about, arms whirling like propellers, the rags at the ends of her extended arms a blur, while the doctor's wife, in her Japanese accent, accused my mother of knowing where all their missing things had gone.

"Here," my mother says again. One hand on the wheel, the other arm outstretched, an offering. "Take a bite. Go ahead. As much as you want." In her large brown eyes, a wild pleading shined like marbles.

My mother's arm, its perfect skin smelling of bleach, poised before my open mouth. I open wide, then pause and readjust my jaw, as if preparing to latch on to a Big Mac, and bite down. I can feel the shifting of her skin and the layers of muscle beneath slipping aside until I felt the resistance of bone. She howls but does not pull away.

When I let her loose, I can see my teeth marks—a set of serrated crescents. On my face, I'm sure, was a look of impatience. On her face, surprise, which shifted steadily and swiftly to disappointment. As if she, too, had believed, and was only in that moment discovering that her body would not be my next meal, or perhaps that what she was able to offer me, her sacrifices, would never be enough to end my hunger, my longing.

14

I settled into spa shifts where I only gave massages with stones. I learned to care for my body in many ways—a diet that focused primarily on proper hydration, alkaline foods, customized supplements, teas, and tinctures. Refuges of quiet. Using the barter economy, I traded other therapies for the massages I provided. I meditated, attended embodied dance sessions, did yoga at a studio and at home, forest bathed, lay on floors with others lined up on mats for gong baths, and set my internal clock to the phases of the moon. I walked to the farmer's market twice a week, and the local food—goat cheese and tomatoes, dandelion greens and quelites, peaches and apples—overtook my mouth with fresh, surprising flavors. I tasted the vitality of the earth. Without really calling attention to it, I had learned how to mother myself in the ways I'd needed.

Still, the physical toll of hours and years spent caring for bodies, using my hands to manage the density of the human form, accumulated and inflamed my wrists and fingers, my neck and back. I would wake the day following a busy shift—a double or triple shift if my bills demanded it—and have trouble rising from my bed, move as if filled with sand, my hands swollen and slow to do I what I needed them to: grip.

I held my pen loosely over the page, closed my eyes, gathered words. I began to discern what could be done in a day depending on when I worked next, later that day or the next day. How would I conserve my energy? How would I protect my hands? What did I need in anticipation of all the bodies and their demands for caring treatment? I pulled in and clung to my writing, my books. I attended readings, lingered around conversations where writers spoke of their vocations, their practice, and wished for a different life.

———

The stones I used in treatments were black, flat, smooth river stones. Harvested and tumbled to perfection. Circular and as large as tea saucers, oblong and as thick as fingerling potatoes or homegrown carrots, as small as mango pits, their shapes suggested where and how to use them. Along the spine, on the muscle of a thigh or hip, across the flesh covering cheekbones. During treatments, the stones huddled in a turkey roaster filled with water kept at 130 degrees Fahrenheit. I tucked them beneath clients and rested them on top. Reaching into the hot water, I would grab the best one or two and run them along the skin, slowly applying more and more pressure. All my clients seemed to melt with the ancient assistance of earth—the help of warmed stone. After a session, laid out on towels on the counter, they shined. In between appointments, I would clean the stones with soap, thank them, purify them energetically with smoke from herbs, check the candle I lit at the start of the session, raise the blinds, and open my notebook.

15

I hold the memory close as if it were this:

"Careful, Ma," I tell her as she grips my arm. Still groggy from the medication after her hysterectomy, the removal of her womb, our shared space, she has to lift her legs higher to get into the tub. I wedge a stool in the middle of the bathtub. Drape a towel over top. Water pools around the wooden legs. She sucks in air through her teeth. The water laps at her toes. It's not warm enough. I remove the plug and hurry the water down the drain with the backs of my hands. I start over with the plug, adjust the temperature. The stench of sulfur is thick. This is water from the well. Its pungent iron smell coats the back of my throat. She slumps over, holding her elbows. The six-inch incision makes a vertical seam down her lower abdomen. Cinched together by a row of thick metal staples, the skin is purple and raw.

"I want you to wash my hair," she tells me. Her copper-colored braid is matted to the skin on her back. She still fights the gray, although the color has gotten progressively lighter over the years.

I've never bathed anyone before. I am an adult woman who won't give birth for another twenty years. Yet here is my mother, as if four years old, waiting. She rests her hands on her thighs. Her breasts hang as if filled with marbles, stretching toward the staples. I'm too gentle, and it's a wonder she gets clean at all. The skin on her back, underneath her arms, and between her legs all feels like an inadequate slip, too thin to keep her inside herself, too thin to protect her from the world, from me.

"I'm cold," she says. I wrap a thick towel around her and unravel her hair. I brush it. She closes her eyes.

"When I'm an old woman, I want you to do this." She looks at me. "Brush my hair." Her gaze is loose, unfocused. Never mind that decades into the future she will have only stubble on her head, a white dusting of it, and she will grow impossibly thin, wheeling around an oxygen tank because an autoimmune disease will compromise her lungs. "I always wanted to have a mother." She continues: "If I'd had a mother, she would have brushed my hair."

I slip the brush through the ends first so as not to pull.

16

A fellow massage therapist tells me about Ammaji, Mātā Amritā-nandamayī Devī. An Indian woman known as the "hugging saint," she has traveled the world since 1987 and hugged tens of millions of people. "Amma" means *mother* in Hindi. Offering comfort from the continuous flow of love that moves through her, she holds each person's sorrows as her own. She blesses those she embraces with ultimate compassion. She is a Hindu guru, esteemed as a saint by her devotees because she has the divine capacity to hug thousands of people for hours, for days, and still function. She will be in a nearby city. Did I want to receive "darshan," and be blessed?

I cringe at the idea of a spiritual leader or guru, having witnessed the potential of religion's persuasive shadow—the manipulation often inherent in getting the follower to surrender, a requirement for membership. The frenzy of herd mentality, the hierarchy of holiness. There are centuries of colonization, spiritual rape, and domination embedded in the institution of the church. Wars fought over "God," genocides. And it continues. I know better. I choose to keep my prayers to myself, to find sanctuary in nature, alone. In any religious gathering, I skirt the sidelines and scrutinize the patterns I see at play. I do not want or need an intermediary or a translator. While I am drawn to the power and beauty of a higher power, I sift all information through my own sense of rightness and sovereignty. I'm vigilant about guarding my boundaries.

Still, I agree to go. Here is this small, brown woman, this spiritual leader and humanitarian, a living holy person. Something I have yet to witness in the flesh. All the divinity I'd been presented with up until this point, in my late twenties, had been male and white. The Black Madonna and Tonantzin (Virgin of Guadalupe), along with other expressions of the Divine Feminine that date back to the Indigenous roots of pre-Europe's matriarchal earth-based ceremonies and spiritual practices, will not enter my awareness for some years.

I respect the protocols. I take off my shoes and stand in all the lines, then sit in a chair and kneel in as we inch closer and closer to Amma. Dressed in layers of white and sitting on the floor, she is smaller and darker than I anticipated. This causes me to smile, my heart to soften. This expression of the sacred as non-white, as a woman, is a necessary inclusion for me. Here she is now. Before me.

A fleet of people surround her—worker bees supporting the queen, bodyguards, her council whispering in her ear, volunteers ready for the signal to tend to her. As I approach, there are those who wipe my face, place me against her, stepping aside as her arms complete their circumference.

There is darkness. There is quiet. The world, muffled. This, her body. Her heartbeat, which I can hear and feel against my body. Her breath travels through her chest into her arms—heat I can sense against my neck and left ear as she chants in a language I do not understand. I felt that she is drawing and casting out that which robs me of my true, undiluted self; my own inner, abundant reserve of joy. An opening is created. It is beyond the room, beyond the crowd, beyond my own memories, beyond my mother's imprinting. I am held there.

There is a force of love both gentle and fierce, protective and nourishing, that I feel as my feet lift from any known bottom, and I float. I'm lifted beyond threatening depths. It's as if for the first time in my life, I feel able to access what it must feel like to be a child, rightly cared for, and attended to.

The positive impact—the love, the praise, the ways she saw and heard me, the care, the support—that my mother provided was built on unstable, ever-shifting ground. It was a daily lottery that I mostly lost but still convinced myself to play because of the few occasions when I won. I could not depend on my mother to listen, to be invested in me, in our relationship, to deliver on promises she generously made. What I could depend on was her inaccessibility. I never knew if she would turn her focus away from herself or whatever love interest she was addicted to at any given moment and shine it on me. When she might lie, manipulate, or stab me in the back, only to make me feel bad for her. What I would've given for a different kind of mother, a different kind of mothering.

Not true.

What I would've given for her to be different. Remade in the image of what I wanted and needed.

Not true.

I did give everything. I gave the whole of myself.

Which of us has suffered more? The traumatized mother who could not live beyond her early years of impoverishment in a family lacking her own mother, handed off again and again, or her youngest daughter, who had to find ways to survive her.

Is this really the question that I long to ask, or is it this instead: How do I see my mother clearly and hold her accountable, while also seeing myself clearly, including myself while keeping her at arm's length and continuing to love her from that distance? And, if only in the peace and quiet of my own heart, send her compassion in my absence? I had learned that love meant giving unlimited attention, giving care. But doesn't that also necessarily include being discerning—whether it's toward one's own mother, mother island, or home country—calling out the behaviors and patterns that make any of them less than what they ought to be, what they could be? Pursuing a more perfect union?

———

I do not become a devotee of Amma's, even if momentarily tempted. I do not join the bright and colorful circus of her army, although in some ways I'm fond of them and their ability to action her vision in the world, to make a positive, lasting impact. The way in which their martyrdom seems to energize them. I don't track her tours or seek the continual endorphin rush of darshan, the blessing of being near her, of being held by her. Rather I place her on what I am coming to understand as my own private altar, an inner altar of the heart.

17

Toward the end of my full-time career as a bodyworker, I would begin massages with the client facedown. Standing to one side of them, usually the right side, I'd wait. I'd attempt to set aside my struggles with my own body, worn down after fifteen years of the repetitive motions of providing massages. The physicality that brought me fully into my body, after years of disassociation, and that brought healing with it—to others and myself—seemed to be less accessible, constricted. I suffered from my own injuries and pain after tens of thousands of sessions. In that pause, I was simultaneously apologizing to the client for any disappointment or inability to fix, to cure, while calling in strength and care, and the measured empathy and protection I finally learned was necessary to practice my gift.

One breath. And then another.

I'd place my left hand on their lower back and my right hand on their upper back and I'd apply pressure, slowly begin to rock them back and forth. Track tension and holding patterns so I could choose the path of least resistance, meet them instead of fighting what they refused to release.

Once they turned over, I would bring the palms of my hands down onto their shoulders, pawing across their upper chest in rhythm with their breath and, as they exhaled, witnessing all that they were willing to release spiral out of them into the room. Rising like smoke. My last massages became a dance influenced by principles of Lomi Lomi, the Hawaiian form of massage in which the bodyworker remains fluid, ever in motion. Except my expression was slower, with just enough momentum to ensure that I could keep going. Perhaps if I had known my cultural traditions at that time, perhaps if my being—physical and energetic— had been stronger, I wouldn't have become worn out. Perhaps if another calling hadn't been begging for me to answer it, I would've lasted. But my hands knew better, more than my conscious mind, and my future self was on her way to rescue me.

In my writing, I always return to the mother. As in the woman who birthed and raised me on her own, a daughter of Aida from Carolina and Aniceto from Loíza, sister to nine siblings, from Río Piedras, orphaned once on the mainland.

The mother as in the natural world that holds and nourishes me, that sustains, that provides belonging alongside other kin—frog, deer, magpie, bear, mangrove, sycamore, dandelion seed, prickly pear in full bloom.

Mother tongue, mother country, la tierra madre, la isla madre, la acequia madre.

Mother as source, mother as feral, mother as healer, mother as storm, mother as curse, mother as inheritance.

Mother as the wounded target of racism and misogyny, mother as the one sacrificed. The one put on trial, the one always on trial. Crucified. Burned at the stake.

18

A car accident led me to massage therapy. The force of the impact spun me from facing one direction—west—around and around until I came to a stop and faced north. I remember the moments before and after. Nearly midnight on a weekday in downtown Columbus, a string of green lights, quiet streets. The car that hit my driver's-side door turned me into a top in the intersection. There was no airbag, only the seat belt, and thankfully that. Broken glass seemed to coat every surface illuminated by the streetlamps, reflecting the turning of red and blue lights. I was taken to the hospital, but I do not remember the ambulance ride. I do not remember being observed. I vaguely remember my stepdad and my eldest sister coming to pick me up, taking me home. My mother did not join them, as she was on bed rest for a heart condition.

Recovery took a couple months, but it felt much longer at eighteen. Chiropractic care and massages became essential. The idea of holistic medicine and alternative care took root in me and would alter how I developed and who I developed into. Beyond anything I could have imagined as I lay in my bed, my whole body in blinding pain.

Another accident—the force of another impact—brought my full-time work as a massage therapist to an end. There was speed and shock, but instead of being in my car, I was in a client's living room in my socks making room for the massage table when a heavy piece of furniture collided with my right foot. There was a walking brace, crutches, and then a cane. After the open fracture began to heal came the diagnosis of complex regional pain syndrome, the decline. The podiatrist, the pain management doctor, the workers' comp employee who attended all my visits. The Feldenkrais physical therapy three times a week, regular acupuncture. Six months, which felt endless at thirty-two, of being unable to walk without support. Longer to be rid of swelling, discoloration, and suffering. I lay on the couch for all of one winter and one spring, my notebook on the coffee table, piles of books like cairns around me on the floor, pointing the way on a difficult path. My nervous system did not remember how to turn off the alarm. Cars passing by on the street, people walking on the sidewalks, the vibrations, the noise, were stabs of electricity. Any sound, any temperature, any light registered in my body as pain. Quiet and still, I sank deep into my chrysalis, yielding to the invitation for everything to change.

The waters so deep darkness obscured my vision, my gaze lowered as I peered into depths that had terrified me—imagined myself vast and layered as a whale. My breath a kind of echolocation, a creation song.

My mother, five states and more than fifteen hundred miles away, did not know about my condition, which meant I did not have to also care for her while I changed shape and disappeared.

19

"I can't sleep." My mother wears an oversized T-shirt. The hem lands just above her knees. "Will you come and sleep with me?"

She is sixty-something, and I am thirty-something. She's staying with me while I house-sit in Santa Fe, which I now refer to as my home, say

I am from, even though I'd only become a permanent resident six years prior. I've set myself up in the living room, on the couch, and have given her the primary suite down a long hallway. Hours before, I turned on the security alarm to protect us for the duration of the night. So far, her weeklong visit has been notably pleasant. What I assume would be normal to another mother and daughter. I've taken her on a tour of Canyon Road; we've been to the Santuario de Chimayó, and to Taos Pueblo. I've given her a massage, and we've been to a Nia dance class at a fancy wellness center called BODY, where we jumped and twirled alongside more than sixty other women. We've eaten brunch at the Teahouse and browsed in the independently owned establishments where artisanal, locally crafted wares fill display cases. I've introduced her to my friends, artists and healers, fellow nonconformists, and cried into her lap when a man I was fond of was interested in someone else. She's acted the part of a mother almost the entire time. I've also maintained the boundaries I worked for years to build. I'm no longer an extension of her, a replica. I belong to myself and to something greater.

Now this.

I feel the pull deep in my belly as if an invisible umbilical cord were going not from her to me but from me to her. A notable change in direction, me the mother, she the daughter. She fiddles with her T-shirt sleeves. On her hip, beneath her long T-shirt, is a small tattoo—the Playboy bunny symbol—from a time when she felt like acting out her freedom and as a rebellious expression with a former husband, and with the church, I guess. I'm offended by her choice. By her inability to see that the symbol she chose also sought to silence and objectify her, require her to perform a limited expression, a binary of femininity as prescribed by the forces of patriarchy and ongoing colonization. Her inability to see the way the dominant culture of her island sought to diminish her, the way the superimposed force of the U.S. did the same, as did the men she chose, as did the churches she frequented, and how she learned to do it to herself. How instead of confronting it, she mastered it.

Without her glasses on, her eyes look naked, oddly exposed and intimate in a way that hurts me to witness. Her short hair, gray and white, is as messy as rumpled feathers. It is early spring, and the house cools at night. I pull the blanket covering me tighter. I can see our reflection in the double glass doors at the end of the living room, beyond which are fruit trees transplanted from the Española valley, which lies to the north, and an assortment of feeders and baths for the birds. Somewhere in the house are two cats, included in my responsibilities. My mother scratches her thigh. We have the same hands. Her toenails are polished a dark pink.

She raises her thinning eyebrows.

I shake my head. No. I will not sleep with her.

Another version of myself—the child that still lives inside me—wants to cry. In this moment, we are both children, little girls, staring at each other. All that she wants and needs, a mother; all that I want and need, a mother. I don't want to take care of her this way. The way I've been expected to since I can remember. I don't want to protect her against her fear, emotionally nurse her so she can be soothed back to sleep.

"Please?" she says.

I'm aware that my voice is flat, distant, as I use all my strength to ward off her invasion and her incessant, unsatiable needing, not exclusive to this moment—wouldn't it be so simple if it were. But her history, our pattern, is lodged in this moment. I want to love my mother. I want to be loved by her. And yet I continue more and more to choose myself. I grieve that it is a choice at all.

"No," I say. "You'll be fine. I'm right here. We're safe." I have become the unwilling daughter.

She turns, but not before I've seen her eyes fill, her chin quiver. I would call it a classic performance, but that would invalidate the empathy I'm flattened by. I watch her step carefully through the kitchen, then listen as she speeds her gait down the hall. Later, when I cannot sleep, I'll check on her not once, but twice. Watch her sleeping, her eyelids stilled as if even her dreams have left her.

20

Far into my adulthood, my mother's endless emotional neediness continued to make her a victim, helpless, in need of my rescue. The stable ground I fought for in my own life would quickly erode in her company. Her overt and implied dependency a way to control and manipulate.

In womanhood, I came to realize something elusive to me but obvious to many—while I came from my mother, I was not her. We were separate, as were our voices, as were our stories. I continued reaching. My reach extended beyond my mother and her limitations—her love, her wounding—to her ancestry, to our original home, the island of Borikén/Puerto Rico, to the language and culture of my grandparents and their grandparents. I separated from my mother and dug deeper into our roots, wanting to understand our histories/herstories better, to fill in a context that helped to make generations who they were, make her who she is, make me who I am.

As I reach beyond myself and beyond my mother, into a space that allows me to hold the hands of our ancestors, an energetic warmth I physically feel, an even larger presence of mothering arises. A presence that I cannot restrict to words of any language despite the new words I learn for female deities in Spanish, Taíno, and Yoruba.

Mother as archetype, soulmate, as vision, as template, as myth, as unknowable. Mother as transcendent. Mother as transcendence. Mother as a universal healing force beyond my own mother's human limitations, far into the realm of the divine mystery. I am included in that unknown. We all are.

I reach for it. I am reaching for it.

"The thing no one ever tells you about joy is that it has very little real pleasure in it. And yet if it hadn't happened at all, at least once, how would we live? . . . Joy is such human madness. . . . The writer Julian Barnes . . . once said, It hurts as much as it is worth. *What an arrangement. Why would anyone accept such a crazy deal?"*

—ZADIE SMITH, *FEEL FREE*

LA ÚLTIMA VEZ

BEFORE HURRICANE MARIA, BEFORE INTERNATIONAL ATTEN-
tion for a catastrophic debt to the U.S., before the earthquakes,
before the pandemic, before my mother went into hospice, a
decade after leaving my marriage, I wrote these emails to a lover. While I
regret the lover, I don't regret what I shared. I read them now as if I had
written them to myself. As if two years after this trip, I wouldn't pull up
my anchor and move far beyond the boundary currents of my mother.

May 21, 2012

Blue in the morning and roosters high-stepping down alleys, passing
rain, blue again, and skeletal kittens scurrying beneath crumbling concrete. Paint peels from the faces of apartment buildings, flowers with
their wide mouths, open and beaconing. We walked the neighborhood
for hours, until we knew the streets, the directions, until our feet had

memorized it all. Ma nurses bottle after bottle of Malta. On the beach, a sea turtle's nest, and a group of dark children painting a mural. When Ma told them what a good job they were doing, they twinkled like little stars. While eating grouper cooked in garlic, I looked over at Ma and felt so much compassion I cried. It was an amazing day. We're having an incredible time. The avocados are big as grapefruits. We're eating them with every meal. Now the coquí . . . You would love the way night sounds here.

May 22, 2012

At night, the other frogs (not the coquí) sound like this: "Está bien, está bien, bien, bien, bien, está bien."

If I close my eyes, I can see the painting Carlos Raquel Rivera did in 1967 called *Noche de San Juan*. It looks like the bottom of the sea. Being in La Galería Nacional made me feel ALIVE, and now I want to paint even more. Five beautiful rooms full of Puerto Rican artists throughout history.

This afternoon I took a nap on the couch and when I woke up, I was full of thoughts of you. I longed for your stories. My nipples miss your mouth. My fingers miss your hair in the morning.

I like to leave the front door open, but there is a cat that keeps trying to come in. We're on the second floor. She squeezes through the gate and meows even after I've shut the door. There is a dog two floors above us that barks at the cat. Even though he is well-fed—a sausage of a dog, really—he seems grumpy, caged to the fourth floor. The cat, on the other hand, slips in and out, thin as a ghost, hungry for so much, but free. What does any of this mean?

Tonight, Mami and I strung necklaces of red beads we bought at a shop. We listened to salsa, and she got up from the table and showed me how her mother used to line up all the kids and dance in front of them. She shook her chest and her hips and smiled. "My mother was such a ham," she said. Earlier, walking down Calle Loíza, she had said, "I think I just smelled my mother."

Could it be that the spirit of her mother, of my grandmother, is here with us? And the spirits of more family members who have long since passed on? There is so much we cannot see.

Mami is filling up, filling in, filling out . . . becoming. I get to witness it. And for me, my deep, deep core is being nourished, and I am also becoming. We've found a rhythm.

She sat on my bed tonight and told me that at a very young age, she lost the feeling of belonging and has never felt it since. This explains so much, and to hear her acknowledge this and speak to it—it's as if her gaping wound has the potential to heal, the proper way, with attention and great care. I am cautiously grateful.

The ceiling fans are a concert of whirling noise. I can still feel the rain tracing my face, my neck, the backs of my knees. Tomorrow will be a day of driving and exploring. Estoy cansada y necesito dormir, mi amor.

May 23, 2012

It felt like some kind of initiation: finding a rental car, renting it, then driving mostly vertical from one tip of the island to the other. Two hundred miles is a long way on a small island. My navigational skills are much better than I thought. Yes, the GPS on my phone helped, but not always. I went to Ponce once, two years ago, and today I managed to get us there and back fairly easily. Of course, Mami was praying the whole time.

Green, green, green hills/short mountains rolling one on top of the other, little houses on stilts, bamboo forests, roadside BBQ. We listened to salsa on the way there, reggaetón on the way back.

We shopped and walked all around Ponce. For lunch we got giant stuffed yams from a street vendor and ate them in the park while a tribe of pigeons gathered at our feet. The breeze was so sweet, and everywhere were couples kissing and touching tenderly. It made me want your arms around me, even more than usual. It's the way it should be, affection everywhere. I watched a grandmother bite the cheeks of her grandson—who seemed about seven years old—in a store selling cheap women's clothing.

Ninety-nine percent of the women wear five-inch heels or taller. Ma says, "Puerto Rican women are four feet tall with nine-inch heels." This reminds me of the last time I was here. Being around all these puerto-rriqueñas brings up all sorts of ideas of what it means to be a woman—how do I express my femininity, my beauty, and what kind of woman am I? It always seems to be changing.

The dog two floors up is barking. Ma fed the stray cat octopus salad, and tomorrow I will not leave the beach for the entire day.

This morning I touched myself and thought of you. When I came, I felt you, I felt us, energy like a root in fertile black soil growing through space and time, down deep into the core of being and union.

May 25, 2012

Pretend this is Thursday still even though it's just before seven on Friday morning, because then this little bit will be accurate and then it will also seem as though I didn't skip a day—

What can I tell you that I didn't last night on the phone? When I was so sleepy. That the beach is a great place to do yoga (I had forgotten this) and take long walks and stare at the ocean until completely hypno-tized and soothed by its rhythm.

I wish it were a nude beach. Bathing suits are awful.

An old Black woman walks the beach selling fresh fried chicken out of an insulated bag. There is a reef a few miles out from shore, so the waves are very tame, but signs warn of a strong current. The sea-weed looks like pine needle spaghetti. Other than that, there's no beach paraphernalia, nothing washing up ashore. No sea creatures, hardly any shells. I don't know if it's because of global warming or if all the sea crea-tures are hanging out near one of the other hundreds of beaches. What-ever the reason, it feels odd, eerie.

So much sun I feel I've become the sun's daughter. Mami's Spanish is getting better as she feels more confident and safe. I like it when we're speaking to others in Spanish because then it's like we work as a team; together we've pretty much got it covered.

I discovered a sweet, sweet little spot around the corner called Kamoli. A funky old house with great organic food and tea, filled with eclectic garage-sale and retro decor and a clothing boutique upstairs. They were playing old American jazz when I was there. After not feeling quite this or that because of my mixed-race combo, and also just being a brown girl who thrives on activities dominated by white culture in the U.S. that feel like counterculture to the Caribbean in my limited understanding and experience—hiking, camping, meditating, yoga, gardening, research, scholarship, and my artistic ways, my writing practice and literary pursuits—I felt so at ease in Kamoli. Brown people speaking in both Spanish and English, playing chess, eating fresh organic food, reading, with their quirky thrift-store, bohemian-style, passionate conversations, hand-painted walls, and yet they were still swaying their Latin hips, moving in a way that was unique unto them, that I recognized as familiar. Somehow, I know you get exactly where I'm coming from.

When we drove through the countryside the other day, all the jíbaros looked like us. That's when it really felt like Puerto Rico.

May 26, 2012

There is a Chinese family from Chicago that moved into the apartment across from us. A young couple and two little kids, a boy and a girl, maybe four and two years old. Below us, a Japanese couple, older. Comic book artists here for a comic book convention in San Juan. I wish there was a big porch we could all hang out on instead of chatting hurriedly in passing while opening, closing, and locking gates, smelling each other's cooking. Children chattering in their own language, classical piano curling up from open windows, the smell of garlic and fried fish. This awareness of each other is comforting, even if we're not hanging out.

It stopped raining altogether. Only sun now. The wind is gone as well.

Mami told me a story about her sister María when they were little girls living at the homestead in Rio Piedras. María lost one of the pigs, and Tío Pedro would not let her and María come home until they found it. It kept getting later and darker, and my ma was so worried. (She's always been a worrier. Her father, Aniceto, used to say to her when she was a girl: "Who do you think you are, that everyone's out to get you? The queen of Sheba?") They searched and searched until finally they found the pig.

Once, there were fruit trees—mango, avocado, lime, lemon, y más—surrounding the home where my mother lived as a girl. There is only one tree left now, a lemon tree. No pigs, only chickens and roosters. Cock-fighting is really big here. They have a huge arena we've passed several times.

Yesterday, in El Yunque, I climbed rocks, skirted waterfalls, watched a falcon play or hunt, not sure which. Hiked and breathed in all the green from above, below, behind, in front of, all around me. It soaked into every pore and settled into my bones. Isla Verde.

At a hole of red mud, my mother and I painted ourselves. Drew bands around our wrists and stripes across our chests. When a woman passed by and asked the significance of what we were doing, Mami said, from a moment of strength, "This is our land. Where we come from. Where we belong. We're marking ourselves with it." I couldn't have said it better.

We returned the car this morning, and I breathed a huge sigh of relief. I had been carrying the weight of all the driving and navigation. It would've been nice to share it more, but it all worked out in the end.

One last beach day—

I picked something up for you in Palmer (odd name). A vejigante mask made of coconut shell. It's nothing like the brightly colored ones made of papier-mâché. It seems to have a presence all its own. Watching.

Hasta, mi amor.

"Your heart is your cosmic center."

—AKUTU IRKA MATEO, TAÍNA SPIRITUAL LEADER

RELIGIOUS/AFFLICTION

IT WAS NOT UNCOMMON FOR CONVERSATIONS TO BEGIN WITH "God told me he wants me to . . ." or "God wants you to know . . ." From that opening, my mother or one of my sisters or both of my sisters would proceed to be the mouthpiece for the Almighty.

"Father, God," their prayers would begin at church and at home. Punctuated by "Yes, Lord," "Praise him," and "Yes, Jesus."

Once started, their prayers were echoed with growing fervor by their listeners, as if the praying were a collaboration, a form of call-and-response.

At church or in my family, there was no tolerance for my questions: Why was God a man, and why was his image that of a white man? Wasn't there another way of believing? Weren't we all pretending to know what was beyond the capacity of our own human comprehension? The existence of an eternal, ever-present force—beyond all knowing, beyond our reality, beyond our intricate planet, beyond our universe, beyond the multiverse, beyond all space and time—seemed impossible to grasp, and the more someone seemed to have a handle on it or tried to indoctrinate me in their religious dogma, the louder the alarm in my mind, the more thorough my interrogation and, ultimately, my rejection.

I was a troublemaker. I doubted. My questions were blasphemous. Even my seven-year-old self understood that there were once many points of divinity. Alive and well within me, she had the same questions I would have as an adult, like why, out of all the Goddesses, we now only claimed one or said, "Father." A line of thinking that made the pastor's wife look at me in Sunday school as though something about me was off, evil.

No matter what I asked or how dissatisfied I became with the overt hypocrisy and inconsistencies, the response was always the same, to correct and shame me for my audacity to reject power from the pulpit. You are wrong. You are a sinner. Confess and ask for God's forgiveness.

"Don't you want to go to heaven? Don't you want to be together forever?" my mother would ask. "Even after we die?"

My answer was, easily, no, but I could never utter that word aloud. How could I hurt my mother so much? How could I abandon her?

———

My mother had one bedtime story in her repertoire, and, perhaps because she did not read me other stories, it made an impression. The books in our home were mostly self-help paperbacks that promised solutions for keeping off those last ten pounds, or for finding and keeping a soulmate—how to think positively, how to have power, and/or how not to love too much. I never saw my mother read them; rather, they were displayed on living room bookcases, among fake ferns and knickknacks, a small rabbit-eared TV, and a stereo that required my mother to make monthly payments for years. But this story she could recite while nearly asleep, comatose from working on her feet all day, struggling to be understood by me, yet another person who could and would reject her.

———

Hans and Heidi had spent a beautiful day playing and exploring outside. Playing hide-and-seek and tag, climbing trees, gathering flowers. A truly lovely day full of sunshine and birdsong. It began to get late, and they realized it was time to return home. They followed the train tracks that wound through the hills and would eventually lead them back to their village.

It was getting darker and darker when Hans, who had been balancing on the steel frame of the track, slipped and got his shoe stuck between the frame and one of the railroad ties. He pulled and tugged, but it would not budge. Heidi thought he was joking, as he was ever the playful brother.

"Oh, come on, Hans! That's enough. Mother and Father will be worried."

It was then that they felt the tracks begin to vibrate. They knew what this meant. Hans jerked his foot this way and that way with more and more effort, but nothing changed.

"Hurry, Hans!" Heidi yelled, as she could see the smoke from the train engine start to fill the air. "Try harder!"

Then they heard the sound of the train screaming as the tracks shook even more. No matter what Hans did, his foot was still wedged. Not even Heidi, who pulled on his toes and his heel, could help him break free.

When I was nine years old, I lay cradled in the meaty arms of Pastor Tate as he asked me if I would accept Jesus Christ as my lord and savior. It was 1986 at the Church of Christ in Canal Fulton, Ohio. I said yes and pinched my nose. My legs went slack, and he plunged me below the cool murky surface of the baptismal tub, washing me clean of all my sins as the congregation watched.

I was the last member of my family he baptized. Not counting the baptism I underwent as an infant in a Catholic church, where my mother committed me, already a sinner at birth, and my life to God. Earlier that year, Pastor Tate had submerged my mother and my older sisters. We had all been reborn.

On any given Sunday, at the back of the church, my mother—wearing red lipstick and a button-down dress that exposed her cleavage—bowed

her head, squeezed her eyes shut, and pleaded with God. Humble, in
need.

———

The message was not always overt, but it was still clear. God was love,
but God did not love everyone the same. He loved white people more,
and that's why they suffered less. That's why they had more, earned
more, received inheritances, were treated better, were the authority on
all matters. But he did love Black people and brown people. All colors of people. He pitied them. He loved Americans and America best,
but not Native Americans who committed idolatry. God loved mission
trips and church groups that dedicated themselves to being of service
abroad, saving people's souls. There were so many souls that needed to
be saved. Anyone could be stripped of who they were, relieved of their
own identity, their messy history, and simply become a child of God. He
had mercy on them.

———

"Ay Dios mío," my mother would say. A Spanish phrase that seemed to
fall out of her mouth without her even knowing it. It was a reaction to
anything, to all things, whether they were shocking or pleasing, whether
she was exasperated or satisfied. A reflex, it was said as one word, *aydios-
mío,* and seemed to serve as filler, a pause that was needed whatever the
circumstance. Despite all the times I heard it, I never became conditioned to say it. Instead, I'd sigh out the word *welllllllll,* or *hmmmm-
mmm,* or *fuuuuuuuck.*

———

At first, my withdrawal from the church and all related activities seemed
to get lost in the shuffle of my mother's fourth marriage and subsequent
divorce, and another depression that kept her barely functioning, this
one a year long. My eldest sister had already been married and divorced.
My older sister had had her only wedding, followed by a marriage that

stuck and continues to stick nearly three decades later. Suffice to say, these ladies were preoccupied. As I edged into fifteen and did my best to survive sixteen and seventeen, my behavior caused a hierarchy of concerns. I would go silent for days and not speak to my mother. I would starve myself for weeks and months. I would disappear at night. My conduct was deviant. I was confrontational in my state of protest, as was evident in the art I painted, the poetry I wrote, the music I listened to, the books I read, the dark circles under my eyes that I only occasionally covered with concealer, my lack of self-beautification or regard for my appearance in general, the unresponsive form I learned to escape to. All of these trumped the status of my soul's salvation for a while. But that changed.

At some point, things settled.

My mother and my sisters—evangelical, fundamentalist Christians—returned once again to the height of their religious practice. This consisted of devotions in the morning, meditations on the word of God throughout the day, prayers before each meal, and periods of fasting, not to mention Sunday morning services, Wednesday evening services, and weekly Bible study. Prayer chains were employed, and there were long, invasive, confessional discussions in small groups or in pairs over the phone, during which God would be consulted through lengthy, earnest pleadings. My family had passed the phase when God was an afterthought, mentioned in passing so as to keep the faith but not be inconvenienced by it. Everyone had recommitted themselves and their lives to God, saved once again, but I had not.

Soon thereafter, the interventions started.

———

God loved men more than women, all because of Eve. A woman tempted a man and led him astray, and everyone would suffer the consequences for thousands of years. God did love mothers and wives, like Mary, and commanded that the men protect them because men were the leaders of their families, of their homes. Warriors, kings. A pious woman, a godly woman, a good woman was submissive and obedient. She did as she was told. God loved white women. Women who weren't white were loved, too, but not the same. And all women were to be pitied.

———

My mother puddles on the floor at my feet, begging. My sisters surround me. I'm sitting in my bedroom, in the home of my mother's fifth and final husband. I've been reading in the corner, in a chair. The book might have been *Our Body, Ourselves,* or about medicinal plants that grew in our area and how to use them for healing, or Thich Nhat Hanh's *Being Peace,* or Alice Walker's *Possessing the Secret of Joy.* In any case, it was taken, lifted from my hands. I imagine that the candles I had lit were still flickering and the incense nearby still crumbled from its stand, a coil of thin smoke curling and gathering along the ceiling. A Friday ritual I'd once been taught by an aunt, one of my mother's sisters, to clear out the spirits who'd gathered in the house throughout the week and didn't belong. It's possible that Sweet Honey in the Rock played in the background on low, or Zap Mama, or Tori Amos. All of it had been interrupted by my mother's and sisters' urgency.

There were the prayers, the cries, the pleading.

Father God, please forgive my daughter/our sister for her sins. Protect her from Satan's influence and bring her back to the family, to your fold, and return her to your love. Make her see that her ways are taking her away from you and all that is good and right for her and her life.

Bible verses were aimed at me and shot, in rounds, that evening and over weeks, months, years. Hands covering my head, my shoulders, my back as I was prayed on, prayed over, without my consent. So many iterations of rape, an act of control against one's will, a violation—physical, mental, emotional, spiritual—were and are condoned in a culture of ongoing colonization. Without permission you are taken over, occupied. My throat closed, the difficulty of breathing when one is held in place, when one cannot leave, when one cannot object.

"Father God, forgive her."

From my chair in the bedroom, looking out at small stands of trees that had been whittled in number to make room for the fields of crops, I glimpsed twilight. The sky cloaked in layers of gray—everything tinted blue. No matter which rural expanse or village or county seat I found myself in, had survived, I was different. I was not the same. I would never be the same.

I'd been forced to learn this through the stares, through the questioning, through the intonations, through exclusion. But now there was more to accept—I was different even from my own family. This was clear in many of the choices I made, but this underlying, unifying choice was the anchor, the cornerstone, the linchpin. The women—my mother and my sisters—who had been my only familiar force in a world where I was continuously othered, were now the ones I had to guard myself against.

I was not a sheep, or a black sheep; I was a goat. Goats were not favored in the eyes of God. Being myself, not what they wanted me to be, not what made them comfortable, not a preapproved, ready-made replica, meant trouble. There were so many ways I was different. It seemed inevitable that I would eventually reject their religion and that they, in turn, would reject me, but it was no less crushing when I had to face it.

Disbelief was a serious sin that had consequences. Eternal damnation.

Interventions equaled a forceful invitation to submit to God and to the authority of the church, which across the United States had become a place to further indoctrinate worshippers into deifying white-bodied heterosexual male authority.

———

Hours after an intervention, having collapsed in bed, gripping blankets for any possible comfort, I dared not touch the edges of my emotional pit, becoming consumed by darkness. I sensed that accepting the totality of these feelings would annihilate me.

In my teenage years, as the baby of the family, I was marked with a choice, an ultimatum. If I chose to be unto myself, my own authority, my own authenticity, to include and honor that version of myself, I was choosing to reject God, to be out of reach of his love and forever under the disappointing glare of my family, who were better, favored by their choice.

I did not even know how to begin to acknowledge the separation, the cruelty—a terrible combination of their ignorance and righteousness—of their attack in that moment, in those moments, but it continued.

———

God loved all children, even babies who emerged sinners from their mothers' wombs. But God loved boys more than girls. Girls you had to monitor closely. You had to make them promise they wouldn't have sex until they were married. You had to put a ring on their finger that marked their loyalty to Jesus until their husband's ring would replace it. God loved boys but not boys who loved boys. God's love was specific, and to receive it fully you had to accept him into your heart as your savior. Then, you had to follow the rules, because love wasn't without conditions. God's limitless love was defined. It was a narrow and tall order.

———

My mother's bedtime story continued,

It was then that Hans and Heidi remembered to pray to God, to ask for help. They immediately heard a voice booming from the sky. It was the voice of God!

"TAKE OFF YOUR SHOE!" he said.

It was at this last part, when God spoke, that my mother would rouse herself, raise her head, even sit up, and impersonate God the Father. With her voice deep and loud, as she had been told and had grown accustomed to thinking reflected any man in charge, she'd say:

And just in the nick of time, Hans undid his laces and pulled out his foot, and both he and Heidi went tumbling down the hill away from the oncoming train.

Alive.

Safe.

———

I never asked my mother the origins of this short drama, unabashed in its moral directive, because I never entirely trusted her ever-changing, evolving answers. But I can hear the voices of the nuns who likely shared it with her during her years spent in a Catholic mission, the place where unwanted children were taken and left. At five years old, I didn't care where it came from. It was dramatic. It had tension. And there was a hero: God. And didn't we need a hero more than anyone? Weren't we desperate to be saved, wasn't that our permanent condition?

The nuns and priests were surrogate parents to my unwanted mother, and God the Father lorded over them all. At the mission, I assumed, she prayed multiple times a day, went to Mass multiple times a week, sang hymns, recited liturgy, and went to confession. Little surprise, then, that in the decades to come, whenever my mother was down and out—poor, battered, single, desperate—she'd return to the solace of the church and rediscover her faith more fervently than ever before. Shelter in the paternal structure of it. This was how when I was seven, we ended up at the Church of Christ, where I was baptized two years later. My mother was going through another divorce, unable to support us—her three daughters—and feeling lost and dejected. This was the first time I remember experiencing religion; for my mother, it was a continuation.

My mother was constantly afraid. I watched as she ran through countless boyfriends and four semipermanent husbands. When things were good, she assumed she was doing right by God, that he was doing right by her, and that her sinful nature was down to a minimum. When things were bad, she stuck her head in her Bible, knelt down, and went about her days praying out loud and praising the Lord. It was in those rock-bottom moments that God became the perfect man, the perfect father and husband she had yet to experience. Held up to this divine example, no man in her life ever stood a fighting chance. She wanted to be loved unconditionally. She wanted a mansion in heaven on a road paved with gold, not altogether different to this island girl than the promise of the American Dream.

While the interventions eventually came to an end, the message continued and would resurface. No matter what I tried to say or explain, the response was always the same.

"But don't you want to go to heaven? Don't you want to be together forever?" my mother would ask.

"Your life would be so much better if you gave everything to him."

"It's all just a dead end unless Jesus is lord of your life."

I wanted to say that I still believed, but in something beyond what I could name or had language for; that I still prayed—nearly all day long, but with attention and connection rather than words; that the graces and benevolent forces of the unseen were all around and active; that I trusted this experience, my experience, without having to control it or have it control me. But there was no space to do so.

I never insulted my mother and sisters. I was never disrespectful in my objection. Even now in moments of fantastical thinking, I can barely conjure a scene where I turn to them with all that I was made to bear—the inappropriate faulting, the devastation of being singled out and rejected, continuously disparaged and demeaned—and scream with all the self-possession and self-authority I've come to know, "How dare you?"

I was alone. Alone even in my family.

It has taken me my entire adult life to unwind the deep conditioning imposed by my mother's need to live an unconscious life motivated by fear and zealotry, a life that on the one hand offered stability and hope, and on the other hand caged her, made her a servant of the Lord, a perpetual dependent, and demanded unquestioning devotion. That stole her away from me. That ultimately fractured my family, splitting it beyond repair.

My family's approach was a model of bifurcated thinking that is one of the hallmarks of the colonized mind. Good/bad. Day/night. Right/wrong. White/Black. Straight/gay. I rejected this orientation, because it hurt every part of my being to act as if this oversimplification of a divine, eternal force—diluted beyond recognition so that congregations could digest it and behave—was anything less than toxic and traumatizing.

That the narrative was wielded to justify genocides of all kinds, horrific histories of violence across the world, that it fueled the patriarchy and condoned enslavement—especially that of the Caribbean, which directly impacted us via the direct lineage to our ancestors—was a point my family didn't see as valid. To me, that point was everything.

———

We have always been more sacred than any cathedral, than the preaching in any church, despite the conquests, despite being coerced to convert. The torture. We never needed the invitation of an outside force, an externalized exported construction that was beyond us—something we were convinced was holy—to enter ourselves, to enter our hearts, our souls.

We have always been, each of us, an altar. Our own fleshy muscle of heart more intelligent than any outsourced authority, our connection to a presence of divinity as implicit in our being as cell, organ, bone, breath. We just needed to remember. We just needed to believe.

.

"*Two or three things I know for sure, and one of them is the way you can both hate and love something you are not sure you understand.*"

—DOROTHY ALLISON, *TWO OR THREE THINGS I KNOW FOR SURE*

DISAPPEARED BY HUSBAND,
PART II

A BANANA AND A BOTTLE OF WATER. HE HAD PACKED THEM for me along with the ones he'd packed for himself. Pulled out of his bag, they were a greater gesture than flowers or chocolates. Instead, here were gifts of potassium and hydration. Needed, useful. I had neglected to bring them for myself. Early October warmth lit the sky, and we'd pulled off layers. After our hike through the glen, we'd returned to where we'd parked in the grass. My jacket now strewn across the front seat, my sweater tied around my waist as we ate and drank, our backs against the cab of his Toyota Tacoma. The leaves of the birch, maple, and oak trees were in the throes of turning and falling. The air around us held a particular mix of sun and sharpness, a warning of the coming season, when the living turned toward preparing for the cold and darkness, as if guarding ourselves against it. An ancient orientation: the need for security as the days shortened and the light continued to fade.

I had trouble deciphering his show of kindness. Did he want to be my friend? Given that he was older—I didn't know by how much—was he looking to be a mentor of sorts, a father figure? Was he already involved with someone else? One of those men who never spoke of his romantic life, never called his girlfriend what she was, never wore a wedding ring? I couldn't tell. In that moment, standing at the cab of his pickup as I fiddled with the peel of the banana, washing down the chalk of the fruit as it wasn't yet properly ripe, I couldn't subdue my insistent smile.

My attraction to him had been lit, and however cautiously it flickered, it still produced heat.

Following our hike, we toured the annual fall arts festival in Yellow Springs—a shared favorite, distinctly different from the rest of Ohio with its lack of big-box stores and fast-food chains defying the sameness and smallness repeated ad nauseam across the Midwest. Suburban sprawl that had me singing Joni Michell's 1969 original version of "Big Yellow Taxi"—"They paved paradise, put up a parking lot . . . / They took all the trees, put 'em in a tree museum"—and Chrissie Hynde of the Pretenders chanting in the 1983 release of "My City Was Gone": "I went back to Ohio / But my pretty countryside / Had been paved down the middle / By a government that had no pride."

Here, in the late 1990s, the veneer of polite engagement by other Ohioans seemed to barely distract from the intense shadow of homogeneity, at the center of which hid a burning coal of white hatred. Yellow Springs was home to Antioch College, the radical outlier. I felt a kinship with those in the community and with the glen, the ravines, the sacred pine forest planted by formerly enslaved women—a church of pine needles, spirit, sky, and air. A place where the divine can truly reside. I had hiked in wide-legged jeans and a pair of 1960s boots I'd bought secondhand. My only layers a thin sweater over a tank top, a worn corduroy jacket, and an embroidered scarf that I often wrapped loosely around my head. He was outfitted in fleece and pants made for the trail, Smartwool socks and day hiking shoes, wraparound sunglasses, his dark, short hair flashing a strand of gray when the sun hit and his head was tilted just right. Our steps were steeped in quiet. We were attentive to the sounds of nature: the river, the winged ones recovering at the raptor center, the wind through the leaves in their concentric dances of letting-go.

That day was the start of a simple, steady, slow-motion seduction. His gifts and his presence—a seemingly gentle, subdued way of being— were in sharp contrast to those of the young men close to my age with whom I'd found myself caught in perpetual games of chase. I distinctly remember the weeks leading up to this outing, walking the small-town blocks to my car after working all day in a specialty gift shop, begging with each step for a suitor, a mate who would appear suddenly in my life with the sole purpose of rescuing me. I was lonely. I was bored. I was living with my mother and stepfather in the vast expanse of rural northeastern Ohio, attending massage therapy school in Columbus on the weekends, staying closer to where we lived and saving the gas and miles put on my Ford Escort during the week to work retail in a nearby college town. Even though I blasted Ani DiFranco's recently released "Not a Pretty Girl" and sang along with her with conviction—"I am not a pretty girl / That is not what I do / I ain't no damsel in distress / And I don't need to be rescued"—nothing could have been further from my own trauma, my own hurt, my own constant and insatiable longing. I was not "a maiden fair," and still, once the CD stopped spinning in my Walkman portable player and I removed the headphones, the aching consumed me.

What followed my devoted bouts of pleading was this man, a court-ship of the mundane, which to me, at twenty years old, after all I'd lived through under my mother's rule, seemed unreal, intoxicating in its con-sistency and dependability.

A fairy tale.

Later, I would point to that simple offering of a banana and a bottle of water and see his forethought and his caretaking as the moment I knew I'd marry him. Like the princesses in any popular fairy tale—or Top 40 song, or rom-com—I'd learned up to that point, I was a damsel in distress and in need of rescue. I had been waiting.

"The Little Giantess dreamed that one day she would find a very fine mate," Clarissa Pinkola Estés narrates in *The Power of the Crone: Myths and Stories of the Wise Woman Archetype,* a collection of audio teachings. "The Little Giantess" was a story told in Dr. Estés's family by her aunt Edna. It begins with a description of the Giantess family. "Once there were three giantesses: one very old whiskery Grandmother Giantess, and one only slightly whiskery middle-aged Mother Giantess, and one very young Giantess, who was as yet whiskerless." My memory of replaying this story numerous times combined with the relationship I've made with it over the years leads me to retell it in the following way—close to but different from Dr. Estés's—my own iteration born of her initial telling.

———

Despite all her dreaming of being wed, the Little Giantess was having trouble with suitors. No matter where she went or what she did, there was little in the way of prospects. Wedding bells rang out through the valley with great frequency, announcing how easy it was to find love. Celebration happened all around her and without her. For the Little Giantess, matches were few and far between. The men that did have the courage to approach her, making conversation as they peered up at her—she towered above them—quickly grew tired of craning their necks, shouting up so she could hear them. Positioned beside her, they could see who was bigger, stronger, more gallant. The men seemed to wilt the more time they spent getting acquainted with her. On the rare occasion that a potential mate lingered and kept the conversation going—as he squinted into the sun, beholding the mountainousness of her—he would be visibly disturbed when the Little Giantess mentioned her heritage, her family, spoke of her mother and of her grandmother.

"If you think I'm something, wait until you see them!" she would say, confusing them with her excitement. Her mother and her grandmother were of course much larger and more imposing, with their massive legs and hips and all their whiskers.

Hearing this, the suitors fled. And there was the Little Giantess all alone again.

The Mother Giantess grew weary of her daughter's struggle, and she offered her daughter this advice: "Make yourself smaller. The way you walk, as if strutting, don't do that. The way you talk, as if you're always asking a question or proving a point, don't do that. The way you dress, all those colors together, more mismatched than any wildflower garden, don't do that. The way you do your hair, the way you ignore your face, the way you smell, the way you laugh, as if you don't know any better about the way these things ought to be done."

The Little Giantess was discouraged and protested, saying, "But I like doing things my own way. My way brings me joy."

"Well, if you want a mate, delight and satisfaction are not the point," said the Mother Giantess.

The Little Giantess thought it over, grew sullen in her unrelenting desire to be matched, and decided to obey her mother's instructions. In the weeks following their talk, the Little Giantess grew tame and tired.

———

He had appeared in the boutique where I worked, Essentials, which sold nonessential things to decorate your house and yourself, all artisan made. In another college town, not anywhere near as radical as Antioch or Yellow Springs, there he was, in a T-shirt with an image that was indecipherable to me.

"You really don't know who this is?" he'd said after asking me to guess. The image was of a man with his shirtsleeves rolled up and arms outstretched, rendered in simple black lines. Something he'd picked up at City Lights Bookstore on a visit to San Francisco.

"Don't you know the Beats?"

I continued shaking my head, my smile growing. I'd transferred too many times—attending a different school each semester for three semesters before I dropped out of college altogether—and missed that American Literature course where surely the syllabus would've required the indispensable texts.

"Kerouac, Cassady, Burroughs, Ginsberg, Snyder." He turned slowly around, stretched out his shirt as if to fully display the image printed on it. "You don't know *On the Road*?" He was pointing now with both hands, his soft voice growing louder. "This is Jack Kerouac."

I did not know the Beats or the Beat Generation, even though the folk music I listened to—Joni Mitchell, Joan Baez, Bob Dylan, all in their early days—could've led me there by association. The computer was not yet king, and the internet was still far from remaking the world in 1996. But this man who worked in the back of a college bookstore, hidden away by cinder block walls, knew books, knew literature, was excited by it. I would later come to see him as the spitting image of Neal Cassady as captured in the classic sepia-toned photo of Neal and Jack Kerouac arm in arm taken by Neal's wife, Carolyn, in 1949. I had dropped out of art school and refused to take my only other creative love, writing, into the classrooms of academia to be eviscerated as well. Instead, I studied massage therapy and sat for the medical board licensing exam necessary to practice and claim income in the state of Ohio. This after suffering a car accident and, in my healing journey, turning to bodywork and holistic therapies to wean myself from a daily dependence on pain relievers, to interrupt a chronic cycle of migraines, and to find the full range of motion in my neck, shoulders, and upper back again. I'd given up on becoming an adult, one who could afford their own place, or a student, or an artist, and settled for practicing a trade— not unlike my mother, the barber. I had recently begun my coursework when this man came into the shop interested in a pair of handmade, one-of-a kind earrings in the glass case behind which I stood. Nature music coupled with the harp played on speakers hidden among shelves of toiletries—Crabtree & Evelyn products and other specialty soaps, scrubs, bath pearls and lotions. This was before the Body Shop and Bath & Body Works became popular, long before you could find Crabtree & Evelyn at Walmart. When small downtowns were still primarily run by individual business owners and their families.

His invitation felt benign; he seemed perfectly safe. We agreed to meet close to the highway and drive south to the forest, and then to the reassuringly funky and countercultural community celebrating its artisans on the streets of Yellow Springs. After the festival, we headed back to our initial meeting spot but detoured to the capital city, where we continued with dinner and a movie. Our time together lasted the entire day, from early in the morning to late at night. It reminded me of the dates on *Love Connection,* with host Chuck Woolery, I'd watched as a child. Parked for hours in front of the TV while my mother and older sisters blew in and out of the house lured by the promise of men, by the power of infatuation, which may or may not have led to love.

It was mostly quiet in the cab of his truck that day, the windows down on the highway, occasional long glances at each other. The calm was a comfort, like the banana and the water. And when the conversation did happen, it flowed easily. I wanted to hear about what he knew, what he'd experienced, and as a young listener, who came to dating late—my first real relationship only two years before—my presence, the whole of my body, was fresh, yielding earth, ready for planting.

———

The Little Giantess was asked on a date, at last, and her mother was overjoyed.

"See? What did I tell you!"

As the Little Giantess prepared to go out, she rehearsed her most subdued form. Pulling a gray cloak off the hook by the front door, she covered herself with it. The hood hid her hair and much of her face. She looked into the mirror and practiced smiling with only her eyes. Remembered her earrings made of chimes and removed them. Placed them in a log bowl on the boulder stand near the entryway. Her grandmother, paying close and quiet attention, got the Little Giantess in her grip and brought her close. Her voice was gravel and shadow.

"Now, you listen to me, little whiskerless one. You do as you do tonight. No censoring allowed. If you see trees struggling in poor soil, you had better snatch them up like you always do and replant them in fertile places. I expect nothing less from you."

And so, the Little Giantess in her excitement slammed the door behind her, tossed off her cloak, let down her matted mess of vine-decorated hair, and went leaping down the path past her suitor, who followed her down the

twists and bends. She stopped now and then to transplant a tree who cried
out to her, and the suitor, out of breath, cheered her on.

"What a great heart you have! What a terrific thing to do!"

Before the night's end, once she had become calm, satisfied with herself
and her work, the suitor turned to her and with a look of admiration and
respect, asked if he could see her again.

———

There was a suspension in the first month, a pause from reality or perhaps a spell, where instead of trying to find out everything about each
other, we revealed personal details only sparsely. We enjoyed being in
the moment with each other. There were indie films at the art house cin-
emas, gallery openings, meals at his favorite restaurants, folk concerts at
cafés and intimate theaters, browsing through bookstores and moun-
taineering/outfitter shops, long hikes, and weekend camping. We did
not tell each other how old we were. It was clear that he was older and I
was younger. His hair was still mostly dark with a few silver strands. His
wiry, small frame still fit from the hiking, biking, and running regimen
he followed. He could've been in his mid-thirties. I could've been ending my twenties instead of just beginning them.

We were too busy fantasizing about each other to look closely. We
fell into comfortable silences with each other and hid in them. At a
metro park by the Olentangy River, surrounded by the bleached branch-
ing bones of sycamores, he pushed me in a swing. My laughter echoed
through the arms of the trees, the little girl inside me relishing this man
as if he were the father I'd always wanted. A man who would belong to
me alone. Not someone attached to my mother, consumed and manipu-
lated by her ever-unpredictable storms. Someone steady, who could lead
the way. I was not like the last woman he'd dated, closer to his age, an
adjunct English professor who was demanding and confrontational, as
he'd described her to me in so many words. I was not white, highly educated, and upper middle class.

There was still some part of me—most of me, at that point in my life—that didn't think what Gloria Steinem and other leaders in the second wave of feminism had professed held true for someone like me. Who was *I* to call out, demand, confront? It was one thing to subscribe to *Ms.* magazine and write political letters of protest. It was another thing, as a young, brown, working-poor woman in small-town Ohio, to deal with the generations of colonized lives in my DNA. When facing my own childhood trauma and lack of parenting, what I was desperate for was someone to love me, only me, and to not disappear. It was my inner four-year-old or seven-year-old or ten-year-old who dictated what I needed, decided my fate. And in that way, my mother and I behaved in exactly the same way.

It would be years before I would understand how to translate feminism—the value of myself, the value of women as equal—into language that held my own context as African Indigenous, as Boricua. Understand what it means to see myself as the ultimate authority in my own life, trust myself, cultivate a relationship with the Divine Feminine. See myself and treat myself as sacred.

He would never be my father. He was nothing like my father—a tall, imposing man who made his life and career in the military. A veteran who freely shared his hatred and suspicion of women and people of color, who barely hid his ignorance around strangers, whose intense shadow of fear caused him to sleep with a gun under his pillow at night, and who married women who could not speak English, were not citizens, with whom he could play pretend dictator, continuing his rule.

It's a harsh character sketch, I know.

And it's here where I don't know whether to detail the few times with him I had as a child when he threw me high into the air while I shrieked, delighting in flight, or, conversely, the times when he pitched me into the deep end of the pool, again and again, as I begged him to stop, my lungs filling with water, or pinned me with his body weight, his enormous hand in my mouth pulling teeth that were not entirely loose in the event that he was not present when they were truly ready to come out.

I want to say it went like this:

I try holding on to my father by the ears as I sit directly behind him in the back seat while he drives, not on his lap, where he sometimes lets me sit and steer. I'm perched on the edge of the wide cushion, its suede-like upholstery kitten soft. It rubs against the backs of my bare legs. I take his earlobes into my small fingers, roll them back and forth, squish and squeeze them. I can see the back of his head through the army haircut. The crude shape of his skull. Then his voice rings out louder than the old honky-tonk playing on the radio, as if it were he who should've been recorded instead—off-pitch yet convincing if in nothing else but volume. Decades later, I can still summon his singing, those songs. Still feel the insistence, his, and the dread, mine, inherent in his presence.

He was not my father. It wasn't an entirely scripted story of young woman/old man. He did not woo me with his financial means, as his income was modest, but he was consistent, he was older, and he did love me. That was enough for a time, as the small child in me grew.

There are contradictions, aren't there?
Always.

At some point, there was a photo shoot. He hired a local photographer, and I found myself at the photographer's studio, being arranged. I wore a white embroidered blouse and stamped silver earrings that dangled past my jaw, the sides of my long curly hair pulled back into a clip, and stared off into the distance in not quite but almost a profile pose. It was a black-and-white shot, meant to be artful. Something that could hang in a gallery, an object.

It didn't hang in a gallery. It was put in a frame for private display.

I was the object. Something timeless in that photograph, by which I mean the way men have always adorned women and confined them to a two-dimensional form. I'm haunted by the work of Edward S. Curtis, of whom he was a fan. The way in which the white male gaze contributed to colonization, art that reinforced othering, the way in which the photographer took away the humanity of Native people across the country by posing them and promoting them as "exotic" material—see feathers, see blanket, see pottery, see buffalo, see eagle. A truncated expression, taken out of context, tokenized, and void of its rightful layers of meaning.

I did not know enough at the time to protest against him or the centuries-old cultural imprint of how things should be for an island girl—a crude but accurate equation:

brown-skinned woman

+ white man

= survival.

The Mother Giantess could not contain herself when she heard how well her daughter's date had gone.

"Things are going to progress now, I'm sure of it," she told her daughter. "All you need to do is keep following my advice."

On the evening of the second date, the Mother Giantess told her daughter not to unleash her giant breath, for the Little Giantess would blow trees and all else to the ground for a better view, opening horizons where she saw fit, creating new perspectives.

Again, as the Little Giantess was preparing to leave, she practiced her most subdued gestures. A woman with a blank expression on her face stared back at her from the glass. She pulled the gray cloak from its hook and covered herself from head to toe. As she opened the door, she felt her grandmother's grip around her shoulders.

"Tonight, draw the biggest breath you have ever drawn in your entire life," her grandmother growled. The heat of her words causing the Little Giantess to nearly squirm. "Do as you do. I expect nothing less from you."

On the other side of the door stood her suitor with an enormous bouquet that towered over him. She stepped out of the cloak, revealing a flash of colors: peacock and pomegranate, jade and saffron. Placed the bouquet next to her ear as it was tiny in her hair and thanked him as she loped down the path.

Later, during their walk, she asked him to hold her purse. A massive thing made of hide and bone that contained her necessary and precious items. He attempted to assist her, but no matter how hard he tried, he was buried beneath its weight. Instead, she positioned it in the path. Stepped on top of it and had a good look in each direction. When she faced east, she drew in a breath so deep the whole of the earth seemed to tremble. The suitor stood back and braced himself as he anticipated her breath's release. As the Little Giantess exhaled, tree trunks bent to the earth, and all else even taller bowed, revealing an enormous, golden full moon.

Again, the suitor cheered at her display. "Glorious!" he exclaimed. "What a tremendous act of artistry!" And he asked when he could see her again.

———

One afternoon after a hike, facts were finally revealed. We sat across from each other in a red vinyl booth at Hunan Garden, a Chinese restaurant flanked by Big Lots and Sally Beauty Supply. A surprise of culture in a strip mall on the outskirts of Mount Vernon in northeastern Ohio. Paper place mats with the Chinese zodiac stuck to our forearms, the animals and corresponding years making a circle, which we traced with our fingers. Hot tea and egg rolls "authentically" made by the Chinese family who owned and ran the restaurant in the conservative rural town. Their own presence and true, complex cultural expression and histories hidden behind smiles, slight bows, and the indistinct Asian-inspired elevator music whining on a loop.

I was born in the year of the snake, 1977. He was born in the year of the horse. He didn't specify. Was it 1966 or 1954? The moments hung heavy between us as I guessed, hoped for one and not the other. His actual age felt like ice down my warm back, nearly enough to wake me from the fantastical state I had been willing into existence.

There were twenty-three years between us. An entire adult. An entire phantom adult who was older than me.

The tea became difficult to swallow. My meal cooled, the sauce congealing into pearl-like shapes on the plate. I wasn't sure how much this mattered in that moment. I couldn't grasp the details of the future. The true weight of our age difference and the impact it would have on our relationship. Would it matter more when I was in my early thirties and he in his mid-fifties? Or when I was in my early sixties and he in his mid-eighties? It was momentarily troubling—ominous arithmetic—but it did not ultimately derail us. Later that day and in the following days, I decided it didn't matter, then went about convincing him of the same. This wasn't a temporary infatuation. He argued that I was inherently unreliable given my youth. The fact that the human brain isn't fully developed until one is in their mid- to late twenties proved his point. And still, I promised him that no matter what, I'd stay. That I was committed and worthy of committing to. He gave me a copy of *The Little Prince* and stressed how when you love someone, you're responsible for them. I didn't have the context for what he was attempting to convey. Love was a power game, love was the eight ball striking and scattering the knowns, love was chaos and insanity, love was desperation and manipulation, love was all-consuming with its extreme highs and lows. I hadn't experienced it, but I had seen as much with my mother, with my sisters. More than anything, I wanted to be claimed.

I refused to admit to anyone, including myself, what it was that truly broke my heart. After weeks of dating, he showed me a photograph of two small children—girls—were they six and nine? Thereabouts. They were his from a previous on-and-off relationship with a woman he'd known for years who wanted children and tricked him, twice, or so his story went, into getting her pregnant. The girls, his daughters, lived nearby and went every other weekend to his parents' house up the road from where he stayed—and I stayed with him—a basement efficiency apartment in a fraternity house he was paid to supervise. The girls joined his mother and father—their grandmother and grandfather—as a family, his family, and he would occasionally pause his activities to make an appearance.

He was not mine alone. There were other little girls who had rightful ownership of him, their father. The news made me despondent. After sobbing about the photo, and the existence of his daughters, I pouted for weeks on end. I wanted him to be mine in a way I had never experienced with my own father, my own mother. I wanted to be the whole of his world as any child rightly expects to be for their parent. In a way that I could never have articulated at the time, his daughters were competition for attention, which, to me, equaled survival.

The only way I was able to move past this difficulty was to stake my own claim to him and to wield that power—almost always at their expense. He was often unavailable to them. I saw this as my win. I was too young to summon any mothering or to consider them as a parent would. I simply tolerated them, with polite distance and a carefully cultivated kindness. Their grandmother continued to be the one who kept them connected to the family, the one they stayed with every other weekend until the elder daughter turned sixteen and could shuttle them around as best suited their teenage lives.

They would never stay in our home, accompany us on trips out west, be the focal point in our lives. An admission that over twenty years later, now that I'm the age he was at the time we courted and a parent myself, makes me sick to my stomach. The grief unbearably nauseating. How simple it was to erase them from our daily reality. But in that moment, first hearing of their existence, I sobbed as if something perfectly healthy—our budding relationship—had been forever maimed, and he held me, apologizing.

Photographs of his daughters were not displayed in our home, but a photograph of me was, that staged moment where I seemed to advertise from my frame all that he wanted in a mate—someone moldable/receptive/yielding, dependent/unsure/unrooted—a rare find, as if he'd discovered me and brought me back from one of the foreign lands he'd traveled to in his youth. And, however unspoken it was, I agreed, and lifted my skirt for all access in our frenzied, instinctual passions. Was I not an oversexed island girl, after all? Wasn't I my mother's daughter, and wasn't that what was expected of us? More heat, more spice, more sex. And if we ever dared say no, it was never heard.

———

In the beginning, there were small but meaningful gifts. A copy of Natalie Goldberg's *A Writer Paints Her World,* which meant to me that he understood me and supported me. He thought I might have some interest given that I was trying to gather the courage to paint again, had unearthed a small canvas and paints, selected an image I was going to use—three ripening apples sitting on a peeling green wooden kitchen chair in the grass of a side yard. Looking back, I can see that it was not so much an acknowledgment of truly knowing and understanding me but rather a perk of his employment—the book was, at the time, a new release that had come into the bookstore. He showed me what he loved, including the landscape, art, and culture of the Southwest, and the casual Buddhism of the Beats. I came to love some of the same things and include them in my life, although my relationship to them was of course different from his; it was my own. Perhaps he meant to impress me with his guidance by giving me Goldberg's book, and it worked. I read it, and then all her other books in the following few years, which eventually led to me finding a student of hers in a nearby city with whom to study and write. I committed myself to a writing practice, along with the sitting and walking meditations Goldberg presented.

There were annual road trips to the backcountry of Utah, Colorado, and New Mexico. There was Santa Fe. There was the one trip east to Martha's Vineyard and our summit of Mount Washington.

Because of his guidance, I fell into the tradition of white, male U.S. writers—notebook in hand while sleeping on the skin of the earth—Edward Abbey, Cormac McCarthy, and the like. They seemed biblical in influence, and for a good long while, perhaps longer than I care to admit, they seemed the perspective that was exclusively correct. Walt

Whitman, Ralph Waldo Emerson, Henry David Thoreau, and the literary decedents who looked like them and sounded like them were the standard. Women authors and authors of color glinted from the margins as if temporal. Never mind the Indigenous knowledge foundational in all of these nature writers' perspectives that was conveniently absent or went unattributed.

When I'd lain naked on his bed, just before he'd entered me, he'd told me I looked like a centerfold. A whisper during foreplay. A compliment that made me feel as cheap as the paper used to print porno magazines, cheap as the staples that interrupted the spread of the naked model's body, contorted for the viewer's maximum pleasure. A compliment that made me go numb, crumple. Later, after showering and snacking on bagels with peanut butter and apples, I'd brought up how much I hadn't liked it, how I'd felt violated by it. He'd insisted that that was not how he'd meant it, that I'd taken it the wrong way, that something was wrong with me for how I'd received it. And just like that, I believed him. All the feminist theory I'd read and spouted, and all the womyn-centric media that supported it, did not make it into the bedroom, flaked off easily with the friction of sex. Ideals that quickly expired when applied to my own body in action with another.

I submitted to his version of truth. It was an exchange. I would be included in this courtship only by denying the contrary aspects of myself.

Weekends staying with him meant enduring the sounds of the frat parties being held upstairs and on the other side of his bedroom wall. During hazing season, I'd overhear the raucous noise of drinking games, indiscernible yelps and cries of boys trying to suffer their way across the threshold of manhood. A violent initiation, a rite of passage that spared no one, especially not the young women pleading in the hall, who on one occasion seemed to be pressed up against the wall we shared. I was their age. I was her age. There was little pretending about the harm being done so close, and still in all my fantastical thinking, I refused it.

And he, the "house father," was responsible, their leader, who was paid to look the other way, turn up the TV, put in earplugs if any of it disturbed his sleep. Now I can easily see how much they scared him— bigger, louder, seething with a recklessness and false immortality he no longer had access to.

"I know you better than you know yourself," he would say. A phrase that was hushed when I first heard it, accompanied by a hint of smile. I'd smile back, because the compliment seemed to be meant for me, but in its delivery it somehow made its way back to him. Over the years, it became the way he would wield his seniority. This one phrase could and would silence me, render me unreliable, even to myself.

———

Before the Little Giantess's third date, the Mother Giantess again warned her, as was her way. The closer the Little Giantess came to securing a marriage proposal, the more her mother advised her, the more limiting her mother's instructions became.

"Do not dance. Do not seem smarter. Do not beat him at any game. Do not show him how interested you are." The Mother Giantess was firm the first time she listed what her daughter should not do. But each time she repeated her commands, her voice twisted into pleading until she was bent over with begging. After all, the Little Giantess would never secure the love of her mate if she didn't know how to conceal and reveal herself in palatable proportions. The Mother Giantess still didn't trust her daughter to fully tame herself in the company of others, especially men.

Again, as the Little Giantess was leaving, she went through her rituals of smallness, conforming to the conventions of how a young woman should look, how she should be. The Grandmother Giantess, as always, was watching and pulled her granddaughter in close so only she could hear.

"Remember this: If anyone tries to cover a mountain with a tablecloth, it remains a mountain just the same. Even if one pokes a finger in one's own eye to block the sun, the sun still exists and burns brightly just the same." The whiskers on her face poked at the Little Giantess's ear and neck. "Do as you do. I expect nothing less of you." Then she looked into her granddaugh-

ter's eyes, her gaze full of darkness, distant stars and the Milky Way in its depths. "Be as you are, and you will be rewarded."

That night, the Little Giantess and her suitor had a long, serious discussion. He told her he loved her, and this she refused to accept. She believed they were not well matched after all. When he proposed, he finally gave her the bracelet he'd been wheeling around in a wheelbarrow, which fit only the tip of her pinky finger.

"I'm so colossal," she told him, as if he needed reminding.

"But I love you, and my love is true," he replied.

"I'm so colossal," she said again, as if he didn't understand. "In every way."

"My love is strong enough and vast enough to care for you. If you are sad, I will comfort you. If you are joyous, I will celebrate with you. There's nothing you need that I cannot provide. I, too, am a giant in my own way."

"But aren't you afraid of me?" she asked him, thinking of her mother and all the ways she'd been instructed to be in order to be loved.

"You are kindness itself," he told her, laughing, and for the rest of the night, he continued to put all her concerns to rest.

———

In the initial months of our relationship, he went away on a work trip— for a second job he had taken to help finance our excursions out west, traveling to liberal arts colleges to buy back textbooks on behalf of a company that would then resell them for a profit.

I wasn't sure what was happening to me. I only knew that I nearly stopped breathing for the first day he was gone. By the second day of his absence, I had convinced myself that I couldn't go on living unless I was near him. This was not melodrama. It was a chemical imbalance of the brain. A disconnection signal not unlike withdrawal from heroin or nicotine.

Now I would say to that earlier version of myself, *Clearly you were suffering from separation anxiety; clearly you were having panic attacks brought on by this state.* But I doubt knowing this at the time would've mattered. I didn't care that he'd simply gone away on a work trip and that at the end of the week, he'd return. He'd left. I'd been left, and the tsunami of that felt experience—mine, and my mother's—dictated my reality.

I canceled massage school and work at the boutique, called in sick, as I did feel physically ill. I drove hours north to his hotel, where I clung to him on the bed like a found dog that'd once been left on the side of the road. Or a child forgotten in a home for too long, who was too young to fend for herself with nothing but the television to distract her from her hunger and loneliness.

The desperation. Then. His arms.

My breath returned to me. As if he were my mother, returning to me, as if he were my mother's mother returning to her. How far back did this wounding go? To her Taína arms? To her Yoruba arms? How many daughters, how many missing mothers, how many hundreds of years of desperation drove the car and parked it? How many generations of longing collapsed in his embrace?

A daughter in need of a mother, a mate, a country, a culture that would claim her.

I was unaware in that moment, in most moments with him, that my behavior signaled something larger and off-center.

———

Once we were married, we fell into a rhythm, as married couples do. Expectation drawing a neat, tight boundary. Nothing unusual when partnership equals ownership. An old contract where the wife is property, to be counted, too, as chattel. My wish to be claimed, granted. Many of our traditions, our routines, while conditioned, were unconscious.

After his father passed, several years into our marriage, there was an auction in the front yard of his parents' house. The tables and boxes full of items his father had collected over his lifetime, his wife finally able to rid herself of belongings that had long cluttered their home, organize what belonged only to her. The auctioneer didn't need a microphone, as he was used to hollering at crowds. It was wholly consuming to listen to him—a real live show—the performance of calling out the items, calling out the prices, the patterned, quickening hollers, tagging the responses from bidders. The speed and duration, the monotony, the urgency. I became winded just from watching. The intensity of the show dipped into my subconscious, struck something exposed and electrical. I grew faint and sat down in the shade of a tree. A life's worth auctioned off.

Years were lived by the season:

Spring—

Removing the storm windows, airing out the house, deep cleaning the rugs, painting the kitchen, servicing the mower, tending to the delicate demands of flowering bulbs—tulips and daffodils.

Summer—

Camping and morning bike rides; long naps and parades; clothes on the line; cloud gazing from a hammock; weeding and bouquets of cosmos, zinnias, purple coneflowers, peonies, black-eyed Susans; cookouts and yard parties; days at the pool and at the movie theater; nights stuck to sheets; storms that turned the air green.

Fall—

Road trips and long hikes, changing out seasonal clothes from the closets and boxes that went soggy in the basement, the raking of leaves, orchard visits—hot apple cider—pumpkin scones, fleece and backpacks filled with layers, lamps turned on earlier and earlier, chicken casseroles, potted geraniums and rosemary brought back in to hide out in corners.

Winter—

Wood delivery, flannel sheets, quilts folded up at the end of the couch, the silence of a neighborhood buried under snow during the night, hiking boots and icy trails, frozen rivers, endless cups of coffee and bookstore browsing, condensation on the insides of kitchen windows, an owl in flight against a backdrop of white. A doe crossing the yard, tail tipped with moonlight.

There are contradictions, aren't there?

Always.

My mother's constant advice to me growing up had been to "blend," and I nearly did—or so I thought. In a Cracker Barrel next to the highway sitting with my husband, his mother, his father, and occasionally his mother's sister, during the senior citizen early dinner hour, in a sea of white skin and white hair, I—darker, different—did my best to blend, as if that would keep me safe, keep change from ever coming, keep a greater knowing at bay. I was a quiet, subdued, hollow version of myself, decorative like one of the knickknacks used to make the dining area "homey." Any sort of unique, authentic expression suppressed. If anything, I looked like a desperate twin of my husband. His clothes were only slightly baggy on me, and I often wore his fleece pullovers, his fleece vests, his jeans, and a women's version of the same hiking/trail shoe. Biscuits, fried chicken and gravy, mashed potatoes, and green beans were laid out on the table, more homemade than if cooked in my kitchen. And in the gift shop, there were endless shelves and tables displaying every kind of item to adorn one's kitchen or bathroom, or oneself, to reinforce the myth of America—for white people, by white people, and about white people, alone.

Throughout my life I have caught flashes of other women of color married to white men and into the great family of white body supremacy. At times, I've imagined a particular look in their eye—distanced, unfocused, like they can't quite see me, their situation, or themselves with any real clarity. To blend, you need to camouflage something about yourself, if not your external appearance, then your behavior, your speech, your thoughts, everything diluted until it loses its definition. And in the act of camouflaging, there is so much that is lost. This assessment does not speak to every WOC married to a white man, of course. But this was the case for me. Still, I never considered this while I ate or wiped my mouth, as my husband paid the bill, as we all climbed into the same car and headed home.

I blended when I made the recipes his mother had shared with me on index cards in cursive, or while I stood in her kitchen as she prepared dishes I would have second and third helpings of—chicken casserole, baked macaroni and cheese, chipped beef and gravy, meatloaf, fried tomatoes, strawberry shortcake, and angel food cake cooled upside down on an empty glass Coca-Cola bottle. She welcomed me, and she fed me. Her cooking was a striking change from the boxed instant dinners I made for him in our first weeks, before he took me to his parents' home, where he ate dinner when not with me and had eaten dinner for most of his life. I thought I was showing off when I'd add frozen peas to a boxed rice or noodle dinner. Cut up sausage as the water mixed with the contents of the seasoning packet and simmered down. These were the dinners I'd learned to make for myself in the absence of my own mother, or anyone else, to cook for me in my years growing up.

He liked to argue with me that my intolerance for spicy food was strange given that I was Puerto Rican. I could not cook Puerto Rican food—arroz y gandules con pollo, tostones, frijoles negros y arroz amarillo con plátanos. I'd eaten it on rare occasions, but it was never spicy/picante. But in the Mexican restaurants in central Ohio, he never went without teasing me when I complained about the heat, the flavor interrupting my ability to eat, let alone enjoy, an entrée; he insisted that something was wrong with me. It seemed that he knew what my people ate better than I did. I had become the thing he studied and scrutinized, wanted to correct.

Despite my strained and constant efforts to fit in, I do not know what his family saw when they looked at me. I could try to sift through memories and other encounters around language and skin color, age and personal context, of aggressions both micro and macro, but I won't. There is a thick rug of kindness that covers what was whispered and insinuated, what was misshapen and ugly, not unlike what hides beneath the American flag, no matter how beautiful and bold it may appear to be.

He did become a mentor to me in many ways—this is how you dress yourself for the outdoors; this is how you pick out gear; this is how you take care of your bike, take care of your car; this is how you behave at altitude; this is the music that mattered before you were born, these records; this is the music worth listening to now; these are the writers worth their salt; this is how you plan a trip; this is how you travel; these are the movies worth watching, the art exhibits worth attending; these are the newspapers you read, the critics you listen to; this is how you structure your day, your week, your year, your life; this is how you move through the world with no thought as to the color of your skin, free from the limits of another's perception. There was a middle America, complete with white-bodied-male access, that was foreign and had been inaccessible to me up to that point—the mundane predictability of the day-to-day was intoxicating. Bills paid, no debt, homeownership, food in the fridge, money in the bank. Shutters on the windows, a garden that reeked of security in perennial blooms, bikes that didn't get stolen, cars in the driveway left unlocked, vacation time, trips. And then I began to drift behind him as he led, all that security having bolstered me. The notebooks I had been filling revealing me to myself, pushing me toward the light of my own attention, threatening to snap any ties that could bind. I was growing.

———

So, it was decided that the Little Giantess and her suitor would wed. Her grandmother fashioned her a veil as long and wide as the river.

"See, I told you that if you behaved," her mother told her as her attendants buttoned the many rows down her sleeves and down her back, "no one would fear you, and a mate would fall in love with you."

Bells rang out for miles, and all of nature seemed to sing and dance as the Little Giantess and her suitor recited their vows.

———

It seems too obvious to point out the layers of meaning within the story of the Little Giantess that are hidden in plain sight—like in any folktale worth its tenure. I came to this tale in my late thirties and held it close for years as it shape-shifted and transformed first itself and then, over time, me—until, like in a dream, all the characters became aspects of myself. Even the suitor revealed himself to be yet another facet of receiving and claiming my own pungent, unyielding, colossal, sovereign self that my mother and the dominant culture, the overculture, were always warning me against. The grandmother knows better. An archetype buried in the ancestral line, she transmits what Simone Leigh, a contemporary American multimedia artist whose work reckons with racism and explores the experiences of Black women, says so perfectly, "To be sovereign is not to be subject to another's authority, another's desires, or another's gaze but rather to be the author of one's own history." For to love and accept the whole of oneself, to claim and take joy in what we've been forced to deny, reclaiming identities that have faced systematic erasure, is to say, "I do." The marriage is to our life's calling, to our soul's purpose, to ourselves.

Initially, I heard this story as the deep divide between how women are conditioned to present ourselves when desiring to be loved and the truth of who we are. I suppose that still holds. At some point, though, that fell away, and what remained was something much larger, ever-present in the overculture: the cultural and historical forces of colonization that are internalized and embedded in the toxic mother figure. The violence of rejecting and betraying ourselves to win favor in another's eyes and heart. The ongoing torment of assimilation, the unending toxicity of it warring against one's mind, body, and spirit. It's the face of sovereignty and the deep wealth of ancestral presence, survival, and strength contained in the grandmother that steers the Little Giantess out of situations that will harm her, that will keep her tame and tired. The Divine Feminine—the power of female deities who reside in our traditional cultures and spiritual practices—comes not through the mother but through the grandmother, who conspires to re-energize the soul and allow its ample knowing, bucking any force of smallness, falseness, and control. The mother as the overculture, as the ruling country of the commonwealth, who dictates how to behave in order to assimilate, in order to have a place, how to perform for access to citizenship.

———

At the wedding ceremony, the Grandmother Giantess winked and wiggled her whiskers at the Little Giantess, and the Little Giantess winked back. As Dr. Estés draws the story to a close, she says, "It would be years before the Little Giantess would have her own whiskers to wiggle at anyone, for any reason. But in the meantime, she would practice being true to the great soul she carried."

———

My notebook says it was like this:

In your dead father's hand-me-down recliner, you watched the National Geographic Channel. Mountain climbers. Your feet bare, toes curled as men hung from ice. It was a summer evening. The flimsy screen door the only thing protecting us from the porch step and our extra-long lot, a yard that took twice as long to mow as any other on our block.

We hadn't yet axed the crab apple tree, its bare branches diseased. I wanted to blame you for that, too. I made a cup of peppermint tea. Handed it to you, your gaze cradling my face. Remote control and a mess of small-town newspaper in your lap. Your hair was so white, and it had crept farther back on your head. Lines on your face lingered long after any expression used them.

You are an old man now, I remember thinking.

That's not why I left you. The pink and white of your toenails, the curl of steam from the tea, all on a summer night. The men on television with ice axes and backpacks as if they were turtles—that slow—conquering the tallest peak in the world as if that would mean something, and you with dead all around you, your father, the crab apple tree, watching the sharp angles of mountain and cliff, the sky, as the men were blinded by all that light.

———

There are contradictions, aren't there?

Always.

I became stricken with day visions. A scene appeared over and over within my inner field of vision and hung there like faint smoke. No matter if I was in line at a café, sitting at our table during dinner, on our evening walk, the same square loop, the same turns, the same streets, the same cracks in the sidewalks for seven years—it was the same vision coming to life, as if from a children's picture book.

A deep, dark wood, and then a clearing, the sun pouring in, a coffin laid open on a table. The sun like a spotlight. Bluebirds flitting in air. Butterflies turning on the breeze. All the animals of the forest gathered in a circle, still hidden in the shadow of trees, watching. In the coffin, laid out as if frozen, a young woman asleep.

Me.

And simultaneously, there was another young woman standing next to the coffin in a red cloak, cheeks flushed, eyes wild and alert.

Also me.

The living one bent over the coffin. Kissed the one asleep, the one seemingly dead.

This was the moment that kept replaying.

I could feel my limbs tingling as if the circulation were returning after they had been numb. I could feel the sensation of sitting up and looking around as if everything had intensified in hue. The air was cool and sharp in my lungs, and with each breath I took, I felt more connected to and more convinced of a different kind of lived experience from what I'd chosen.

There was a clear choice to make—stay the same or emerge and transform.

How long had I been asleep? When had my marriage become my tomb? All that safety and security I'd once craved now threatened to bury me alive.

"What do you think love is?" my friend Christie asked.

We sat side by side in chairs facing the triptych of dining room windows, drinking ginger tea. It was raining again, and the leaves on the trees in the backyard were slow to begin their change of color. I watched them and the limbs they hung from bend beneath the weight of so much water.

I'd met Christie years before at an intimate Irish music concert where she'd played flute. She'd had trouble standing and playing. When she'd tried to sit and play, this also seemed to cause her trouble. After the set, I'd asked if she was receiving any bodywork. I gave her my card. We became friends, and while she was nearly my mother's age and offered wisdom only her lived experience could provide, there was a sense of kinship between us. We shared our perspectives as creative women who saw the world beyond the limitations of the overculture. I'd known her as long as I'd been married. I didn't spend much time with friends close to my age while I was married. They were finishing college, starting garage bands, traveling the world, and moving in with people they'd soon leave for others. I felt like a 1950s housewife and kept company with a handful of women who could've been my aunties.

Christie had come to visit me while my husband was away on a book-buying trip. I held off on communicating to her how badly things were going, how they seemed to be crumbling. He'd forbidden me from meeting other men for coffee or for lunch. It didn't matter if they were teachers or other writers, or that the meetings were professional. He grew intolerant of my writing and the attention I gave it. He wanted me to go back to school and study nursing. Writing was a silly hobby, and massage therapy wouldn't pay for my retirement. He didn't like the colorful fitted clothes I had started wearing that veered away from his understated style. He didn't like how I disagreed with him. He didn't like how short I'd cut my hair. I was twenty-seven. He was fifty.

As a horsewoman who played Celtic music with Gaelic lyrics, Christie possessed an eternal song line that felt evident in the quality of her presence. She was convinced of the divine in all forms of life and didn't seem to scare easily or criticize quickly. Rather, she seemed to draw close and try to truly see the complexity in any situation.

She huffed in response when I alluded to the challenges I was facing. "What do you think love sounds like? I mean, what does it say? What are the words it uses?"

I'd never considered such a thing. The granular detail of a word used for anything and everything.

"How does it behave?" She wound the string of her tea bag around her index finger. She sounded impatient and irritated—not with me, but with him. She'd seen us together; she'd listened for years to what I thought had been good times, a normal married life. Perhaps in this instance she could not control her tongue. It seemed something had been unleashed, and it had the bite of having lain in wait for some time.

"What does love *look* like, to you?"

I wasn't sure if she was waiting for me to answer. I sipped my tea. It stung cold and pungent in my throat. "Not this," I finally said.

———

For the first time, I sought out therapy. In my counselor's office, I tried to explain how I felt I'd broken my marriage—shattered it into countless pieces. I was shocked to experience how fragile it was. I assumed all the blame. I was behaving foolishly. I was erratic and unpredictable. I'd changed. I'd betrayed him by changing. He'd told me so on numerous occasions.

What had happened to the woman he married when she was twenty-one? Where had she gone?

When would therapy fix me?

Meanwhile, in the basement, on a three-by-three-foot wooden platform, I practiced flamenco. Sevillanas and a short, choreographed piece my instructor had taught me. I went to private flamenco classes after therapy. The classes took place in my instructor's home, where she and her husband, the guitarist, who played in a corner of the empty dining room, would yell and scream at me to open my chest, pull back my shoulders, and stop holding back, as they sensed me doing from the moment I walked in their front door. An unapologetic force of being. My own presence. They yelled all the jaleo they could to provoke and support me, until we would break into fits of disruptive and rebellious laughter. The music would stop. The dancing cease. Then I would cry while they held me, as my body remembered that my feet have always known and belonged to the loving pull of earth and that my hands have always been held by the magic and mystery of the cosmos, as I remembered belonging to freedom, the pleasure of flight.

———

My grandfather once told my mother, "Never bring home a man darker than me." She said the same to me, only in different words, when I was a young girl, years away from beginning my cycle, much less holding a boy's hand. I told her, "I want to marry a Puerto Rican man." As if I were promising something of value that would please her, impress her, bind me to her even more. She'd been ironing clothes, her hair wet and tightly coiled at the roots untouched yet by relaxer, her face more stubbornly creased than the blouses wadded up in the hamper at her feet. She paused and held the sides of the ironing board while the iron still spitted and steamed. She lowered her head as if she were looking over the tops of eyeglasses absent from her face. "Don't. You. Ever," she said with quiet intensity, then went back to her pressing. The collar and cuffs of her white blouse taking the force of the heat and, under her weight, surrendering.

There is a generational pattern—call it a family legacy, subtle island propaganda influenced by imperialist owners—of always pairing with the lighter option. I've tried it, too.

Love me.

If you say, "I do," does that make me the same as you? Does that increase my price? Make me worthy chattel? A good investment? But who is profiting? A wife must be especially beautiful to rise above her color. Beauty branded onto her surface. Between sheets at night, your skin glows. Taste this: We are nothing alike.

Mejorar la raza. Make sure the children are always lighter. This can be spoken or unspoken, no matter; it is still stubborn conditioning.

For my mother, there was no other choice. White men had money, jobs, were strong—which is to say consistent—owned their own homes. She leaned on their predictability like she leaned against the bathroom wall when she brushed her teeth, closing her eyes, drifting far away, taken by the current of her thoughts. If/when that white man failed to deliver all that was assigned to him, there was sure to be another who'd used his privilege more wisely. He would be chosen next, and my mother would shelter in the proximity of his privilege and all that he could provide. There were years of white suitors, and the last, fifth, white husband. The children are always lighter. My sisters are those children, but I am my mother's mirror image. A day comes when I promise not to date white men anymore. It is not a promise I speak aloud. I don't know whom I'm promising.

The last time we were in Yellow Springs together, we ate at the Winds, a restaurant and bakery that served farm-to-table artisanal fare long before such a thing had been officially named and promoted in eateries across the country. A local artist's work was hung on the walls with the attention and quality of an upscale art gallery. We sat at a two top by the row of windows looking onto the main street, Xenia Avenue. Because my back faced the direction of the people marching up the street, I did not know, could not see, that the crowd had thickened. While I could see a few people with signs, I could not make out what they read. Suddenly, there were more and more bodies, there was shouting, and then everything went silent, everything went still.

In my peripheral vision, I saw a flash of white. I turned as if moving in cold oil. On the other side of the glass pane, a shoulder, in a white robe. Then, the tall white cone hat, which covered the face. Everything but the eyes. In the road, on horseback, the Grand Wizard. I searched for my husband and saw him seated across from me, where he hadn't moved, also watching as he'd seen them approaching. He chewed his food.

"Why do you look so scared?" he said, with a strange smile meant to reassure me. "They aren't coming for you."

The growing crowd became cacophonous as those protesting the KKK's march down the streets of Yellow Springs grew more intolerant. Uniformed police officers appeared and mixed into the crowd, and those in the white robes soon picked up their pace. All of them now rushing past my vantage point from the window, from the table, from the chair. The animal of my body panted. Each hair on my neck pricked. My throat swelled, the food in my mouth hard as stones; my eyes widened and squinted in quick succession as if trying to see—I both needed to know and did not want to know—exactly how far the distance from the rope hidden in their hands, how many steps to the back door, how many miles from the tree they'd chosen, how far to freedom.

By fall of that year, 2004, after nearly eight years together, I would leave.

There are contradictions, aren't there?
Always.

He was always afraid I'd leave him for someone else, someone younger. And in many ways, his fear manifested. The stronger my self-expression, the tighter the control of his reins. In the end, I did leave him for someone younger.

Me.

Writing became my extramarital affair, and perhaps that's why he grew to despise it. No longer did I look to him to guide me. No longer did I trust his reality over mine. I was often left breathless after spending hours in my notebook, coming into contact with my own experience, with my own mind. I touched beyond what I had been conditioned to imagine, into unknown wilds. I claimed ownership of myself—no longer a wife, no longer chattel. My writing, my voice, seared with naked honesty and vulnerability. I was enlivened, electrified at times, by my own total and complete attention. Nearly twenty years after the end of my first marriage, my eternal devotion remains. An unconditional love. The giving and receiving of my own presence, page by page.

This is what it will take me the rest of my life—and possibly the lives of my children and grandchildren as well—to learn: What we know as ongoing colonization resides far beyond our intuitions of power. Internalized, it restricts us at the level of our imagination, at the level of the heart, in whom we allow ourselves to love. And if we are able to include ourselves in our own expressions of love, if we are able to, as women, wed ourselves first, rely on our own authority, knowing, perception, and intuition, accept and trust ourselves and the circumference of our mending heart for the sovereign force it is, then, *then*, what is given in exchange is a life worthy of our living.

*"Convivir: To be in relation with each other
across a long span of time."*

*"Cara a Cara: To see each other's faces, to know the truth
of our experiences in each other's gazes/eyes/faces."*

—DR. ANA-MAURINE LARA AND DR. ALAÍ REYES-SANTOS OF
BOHIO CIBANANI ON "THE VALUES THAT UNDERGIRD AN
ETHICAL CODE OF CONDUCT AMONG THE HEALERS," IN
*CARIBBEAN WOMEN HEALERS: DECOLONIZING KNOWLEDGE
WITHIN AFRO-INDIGENOUS TRADITIONS*

MOTHER TONGUES

SOMEWHERE OVER ARIZONA, IN THE BACK OF A PLANE, TWO old women filled the seats beside me. Next to the aisle, I cast my eyes down as if studying the shoes in nearby rows. I had watched the women closely when I'd boarded. They wore bright, billowy cotton sundresses embroidered across the chest. Their black and graying braids swinging across their lower backs. Short sleeves revealed loose skin that hung down from the undersides of their arms despite the colorful shawls they wore.

They spoke only in Spanish.

I had never been to California, nor had I ever been in the company of Spanish-speaking people who did not also speak English. It was only the second time I had ever been on an airplane. I'd just turned fifteen and was traveling to visit my eldest sister, who had been studying Russian at the Monterey Bay Defense Language Institute. A Russian linguist for the United States Army, she loved languages but did not speak our mother's first language. My mother wanted me out of the house so she could be thoroughly depressed with her new husband—the golf pro with the terrible posture who tried to replicate Kevin Costner's performance in *Dances with Wolves*.

The women unwrapped food—soft yellow corn tortillas that smelled of lard and spices. Broken bits of pork tamales and red chili stained their creased hands. I listened to them speak their language. Seeing them offered comfort and nourishment, the knowledge and familiarity of culture and language evident in their display. I was set apart, and in that distance was a kind of longing, failure, and hollowness. A need for my own stories. I viewed the rootedness of these two as a form of protection from a dominant culture that did not privilege them. I imagined the connection to their ancestors whole and intact given their ability to use the same words, the same phrases. They seemed to be undeniably who they were. They stood out against the rest of us, who blended into one another with our monochromatic clothing and language. As they ate, I listened to the soft, warm sounds filling their mouths, a song. The melody of it.

The only time I heard my mother speak her language was on the phone, in the privacy of our home, behind locked doors and windows, where she was out of earshot and safe. She did not have the same confidence and ease around her mother tongue that the two women on the plane from Phoenix to San Jose shared. She was not protected by a link to ancestry. Instead, she required bolts and walls to protect her from the shame of disconnectedness, contained by and within the overculture. The legacy of U.S. English-only policies in government institutions landed on my mother as punishment and continued its impact on my own tongue, my own ears.

I tried to separate myself from the women on the plane, peel myself away as if a husk. I was afraid of the potency of their difference. It was something I wanted to be included in, claimed by, something I yearned for, in fact, but I gave in to the fear instead. A general but pervasive fear instilled in me by my mother's surrender to assimilation, her belief that to reflect one's origins, to emphasize oneself as a person of color, as a person from the Caribbean diaspora, was to draw direct public attention, putting oneself in the crosshairs of racism. My torso bent into the aisle along with my legs and feet. The flight attendant made her way toward the back of the plane, snapping open cans of ginger ale and Diet Coke. I could see her considering my awkward shape. The baby two rows in front of us popped her head above the seat and jammed her fingers into her rosebud mouth. Black eyes watching.

At some point, the two women turned to me, their faces welcoming and tender as I watched their wet lips bloom with Spanish words, their tongues speckled with crumbs of tortilla.

If only I could've spoken to them of their beauty, acknowledged their value to me. If only I could've laughed with them.

"I don't speak"—my stammering barely audible and filled with shame—"Spanish."

They fell silent. The younger of the two said something to her companion. I shifted in my seat, unable to escape their stares. The elder one, seated next to me, placed her warm doughy palm on my forearm. She closed her eyes, tilted her head back. In her nostrils, an abundance of hair that made me think of elusive feral creatures—dark and stubbled in fur. Spanish poured out of her mouth and flowed over me. I'll never know what it was that she said.

I did not learn until a decade or so later that there was a phrase, a protocol for the tradition of being blessed by the elders in one's family. I did not know as a teenager how to say "bendíceme." But my need to not feel lost, a mystery to others and to myself, was so great that I would have considered asking strangers to bless me, as if that would make them kin, as if that would moor me to their strength.

What did they see when they looked at me? I wonder if they perceived the shape of my body bent away from them, my posture, as a symbol of an internal distortion. So strange and awkward in my own skin, a stranger to the connection offered by sister cultures sharing the same language, as if I were yet another souvenir of conquest in U.S. history. Still, I received their kindness as a blessing, for this girl becoming woman, unable to stand in the entirety of herself. They shared their wisdom and protection for a moment, skin to skin, spirit to spirit.

———

You filled my mouth with water, my ears with water in my mother's womb—her thoughts, her dreams, all that she felt swam through me, merged with my cells, mi vida. A consciousness in words, con una palabra y una más. A song sung, a song singing through existence. My mother, her mother, her mother's mother and on the liquid note goes— carried. My tongue learned to recognize a sound, not the word, not the definition. It was receiving you in private, in secret, intimate as bare feet on the kitchen floor, bewitching hours when sleep and dreams of shores left us. *Agua,* not *water.* You were never hard and sharp; you flowed. Open at the beginning and end, you were always in motion. Carried on the currents of my mother's voice, two words she never submitted to English: *agua* and *mi'jita.* A sound, a song, an ache, a place that encircled me, shaping words unknown but accepted. You were my name. You call me when she calls me. Out of all her daughters, I am "mi'jita." For years, I hear this name nowhere beyond the island of our family, from no other mother, for no other daughter. It is ours. Hers and mine. Three syllables braid the pulsing cord we share. My heart understands your meaning, my heart that feels but cannot speak. You call me when she calls me. I belong nowhere but to her and to your soft song. Each time it is sung is a moment of being held, claimed, submerged in what I cannot contain. The life of my mother, the waters of my mother, the mother of oceans, which I receive into my own waters, onto the shores of my own life. I, the daughter beyond any border of language. En español, solamente. Mi'jita.

———

Is this how it happened?

When the Spanish packed for the trip, supplies, changes of wardrobe, and bottles of wine were loaded into carved wooden chests. They neglected to include their women. The women were left in Valencia and Barcelona, bent like paper dolls into seated positions, hinged to the edges of chairs, pressed flat and displayed on beds of silk and lace.

The Spanish were not like the English, who wadded up their women, put them under one arm, and went about their colonizing. No, the Spanish men, after months at sea, arrived in rat-infested ships, as horny as the day they entered the gates of puberty, only worse, as they were grown men possessed by the frenzy of conquest, of any kind of control, the sharpest of their swords between their legs, swords that they stabbed deep into the native women—Taínas—who, unlike their Spanish sisters, had bodies that worked of their own volition, legs that could run and leap, hips that twisted and rotated, heads that turned to see things exactly as they were. They were not dolls. They tried their best to fight, but still, their legs and arms were bent into positions unnatural to their joints. *If a woman is not a doll, how do you bend her into submission?* the Spanish must have wondered (do most men secretly wonder this?), even if only briefly before they forced their weight, popping joints out of sockets, twisting off heads. And one must not forget about those chained and rotting in the belly of Spanish ships for months while the men stood on deck looking out into the distance, making predictions about the future and pissing into the sea. The African natives—Mandingo, Yorba, Bantu—who had been stacked head to toe with great efficiency to accommodate as many as inhumanly possible.

Any woman not Spanish, not European, a savage.

Wild and dark.

They were scantily clad and crouching with their hairy pockets of sex unfolded toward the earth, invoking spirits that need not be named, remembering ancestors, birthing, being birthed/rebirthed. All this while swallowing the milk of the moon, babies real or imagined, offerings of creativity tied to their backs, singing into seeds and gourds and shells.

The church waved from behind the cross, condoning it all. Conquistadors increased their force, severed voice, severed breath. Their sicknesses spread.

"Peace be with you." Clergymen blew kisses at the genocide. Between verses of "Hail! Father, Son and Holy Ghost," hot irons stamped the foreheads of the enslaved, both African and Indigenous.

Now, more than five hundred years later, look at my face. What do you see?

———

I invite you again, but you refuse to stay. Vuelve. Look at me when I tell you te quiero. Instead, you lean farther away, just out of my reach. I try to hold you in my mouth, but you insist on dissolving too quickly, before I can even shape you into sound. Before I can express myself, before I can be heard, you're gone again. Stop teasing my ears with this seduction that goes nowhere. You were in me, of me, once. Now look how far you've gone. Miles and miles away, beneath other stars, across other oceans, to where millions of other mouths mock me with their ease. Give me one perfect dose that coats my tongue. Everything brightens with your expression, flushes with vitality, blooms into fullness. This is the way it should taste. This is the way it should feel. This is the way it should sound. Every part of my body wants you. And yet here we go, round and round again.

Como se dice?

No entiendo.

Repita, por favor.

But we are more intimate than the combinations of these consonants, these vowels, than the sound created as it speaks into the void, conjuring. A vibration, a resonance. Curled like a seed in wet darkness as it starts to sprout, another grandmother's tongue parting lips, and there is me.

———

I hold the memory close as if it were this:

In the ninth grade, in small-town Ohio, Señora Miller taught the Spanish class how to roll their r's. She was stocky with cropped white hair, a thick jaw, and a short neck. The hems of her shapeless dresses floated around her ankles; her flats were round at the toe like a toddler's shoes. She had been a tourist in Spanish-speaking countries, and sometimes her accent and her attire reflected this. Something bright, something embroidered.

"Clase," she said. "Repitan, por favor: carne, carro . . ."

I was the only student in the class whose mother's first language was Spanish. I was the only student in the class who was not white.

Señora Miller spoke more Spanish to me in the first nine weeks of that grading period than my mother had in fifteen years. Still, my tongue did not need instruction on how to roll my *r*'s. When I was called on, they tumbled out perfectly, as if they had been waiting since my birth to show off. They put Señora Miller's *r*'s to shame. She stared at me with a tight grin, tugging at her silver clip-on earrings with her manicured fingernails.

The class was stricken by silence, except for Davey Smith's perpetually congested breathing, a thick static in my ears. Stephen Johnson, hidden in the corner, bugged his eyes out at me, pulled down his bottom lip, used his tongue to make a top lip—a gross exaggeration meant to mimic my own set. The class erupted in laughter. Fingers pointing, fleshy little knives. I was the odd one who knew how to pronounce words in Spanish but didn't know what they meant. I was the joke, not unlike my mother, who in 1959, fresh from Borikén, sat in a classroom, puzzling over pages of English text, trying her best to finish first, as she thought that was the point of the game. She'd rush to the teacher's desk and watch as every answer was circled with red pen. Then she'd strut back to her desk with the carcass of her test, bloodied by red ink in her hands.

"How stupid," she would comment when telling me the story, laughing. "I mean, I was so stupid."

Even though it was more painful than amusing, her giggling was infectious. I would ask her for help with my Spanish homework, quizzing her on vocabulary. Her English was without a hint of an accent, but when she spoke in Spanish, there were beautiful and surprising fits of sound.

"But how do you spell it?" I'd ask her.

She'd shrug.

"What does it mean?" I'd ask her.

She did not say, *I did not go to school until I came to the U.S.* She did not say, *There are different kinds of Spanish influenced by region and by the people and languages it subsumed.* She did not know to say this.

The sigh, the innocence and desperation distorting her face as if she were nine years old again. For the rest of her life, she would always believe herself to be that stupid little girl who can't learn what she most needs to know.

The words I had to learn the English translation for: *bobo, caca, carajo, culi.*

There's another kind of language test with a white man's mother. The mother of the man I pledged to love at twenty-one, whom I cannot bring myself to call anything other than "his mother" no matter how fond of her I become. The tests are always the same, whether they are from Spanish or English speakers. Prove yourself. One evening, after his mother had made a meatloaf dinner and we'd stuffed ourselves and washed and dried the dishes, we fell into a conversation about food, about the Southwest, about the Spanish language.

"Do you speak it?" his mother asked me. I cannot describe her look. Was I known or unknown to her?

"I can, some," I said, already feeling the hot sting and prick of shame covering my body—the shame of not being fluent and the shame of being different from them. Both were perpetual states of failure.

"Speak it," she said. "Say something."

Born in 1926 and originally from Missouri, with daily behaviors still impacted by her memories of the Great Depression, she was intensely lacking in exposure to and knowledge of the Spanish language, or of any cultures that spoke it. A kind and generous woman, albeit ignorant of realities beyond her own, she meant no harm.

I could've made a joke, I guess, or given a thoughtful but brief excuse, but I felt so small there, in her kitchen, as if I were looking up at my first husband's family from the bottoms of their shoes. How do you explain that as the felt experience of oppression? A smear on the bottom of their shoes—how much smaller and more nonthreatening could I have been?

I had attempted to blend into the family, with charcoal cardigans, casual slacks, modest earrings that didn't extend beyond my lobes, and my recent haircut—a straightened blunt bob with bangs—desperately trying to emulate my husband's sister, who was a good twenty years older than me.

Instead of laughing off the microaggression, I responded in earnest. I pulled out a phrase that I remembered from high school five years before, "Vamos a dar un paseo."

"Huh?" she said, snickering.

"Vamos a dar un paseo."

Let's go for a walk, as in let's leave this place where we are and find someplace else, as in let's allow our bodies to move us, to carry us beyond this moment, this room, this house, this neighborhood block, this question, and in our gaits take comfort that there are some things that we simply know how to do. Some things we will never forget.

She looked at me closely, the corners of her lips still curled, and asked for more. I thought of my sister's husband, who had learned Spanish in rural Indiana and could produce the following phrase just like the recording that had been played in my school, years and miles away: "Una Coca-Cola, por favor, y un café." Training for high school students who would become tourists, who would need to be served.

When my voice seized, my eyes searching the dirty dishwater for soap bubbles, she looked at her husband, then her son, shook her head, and, as if I weren't there, said, "She doesn't know how."

There comes a time when you are everywhere, with lovers, with friends, on street signs and billboards, beside the English on all packaging and public notifications. In my home, on the radio, in the songs I hum, in the poetry I read, in my prayers in the high desert of the Land of Enchantment, where I live, and on my mother's island, la Isla del Encanto, where I return. You brush up against me, wrap your tail around me, force my hand to meet you. Insist on being held. Everyone knows someone like me, a fumbler, a wounded tongue, who can understand what's being said but is quiet, slow to respond. Who tries to hide in plain sight. Who still feels the punishment, the torture, who cringes at the expectations, the anticipation of having to perform. Who can never remember, no matter how many conjugations later—past tense, present tense, future tense; verbs ending in *-ir, -er, -ar;* regular verbs; irregular verbs. Spanish-speaking families in the U.S. and in the diaspora are full of them.

Look at us together, a fondness. Intimacy. Underneath everything I thought you were, there are surprises—Arabic words, four thousand accounted for. Not to mention all the Native languages. What else are you concealing? What else has been obscured?

On the island studying Spanish, I befriend another nontraditional student, una colombiana. We share a dorm suite. During the day we walk through the rain, lose our flip-flops in puddles, and she tells stories of snakes. What to sing, how to move when crossing a river so as not to draw them to you. At night she speaks Spanish to her Puerto Rican husband, who is stateside with their two young children. We start to copy each other. She rolls her pant legs in wide cuffs above her sandals; I slick my hair back. We order the same meal from the same pickup window, echo each other's laughs and gestures. Then, I abandon her for my notebook, retreat as I struggle with wanting to write about the overwhelming experiences en la tierra madre more than I want to have the experience itself. To be captured by a moment or to capture it. Decades later I'll understand how they both exist, one inside the other intrinsic as breath—the inhale and the exhale.

En la biblioteca de la Universidad de Puerto Rico, not one word of English. The more stories, the more books, the more history, the more resistance. Before cell phones were all-knowing, I thumbed through card catalogs, opened one universe bound in hardcover after another. Lost. Found. Lost. I tried to speak like my mother, phrases meant to command, words half swallowed, broken and remade words, a kind of Spanish creole. I have to keep myself still when I recite "Danza Negra" by Luis Palés Matos. It's a memorization assignment from my language instructor, a practice of enunciation. The words produce a percussion, activate music. The poem is an instrument that plays my mouth. My face flushes with blood; my tongue remembers how to dance.

———

In her 2023 interview with Tom Power of the podcast *Q*, Cree inter-disciplinary artist Christa Couture shared what her language coach, Charlotte Ross, expressed to her. Couture, committed to learning Cree but unable to include it in her life in the ways she would've liked, wore headphones in the recording studio as she laid the audio track for the animated series based on her memoir, *How to Lose Everything*. In her ears, the voice of her language coach feeding her one word at a time. Ross shared with Couture their Indigenous cultural understanding of "a language spirit residing within you, in your blood somewhere—no matter who you are," and that "any time we spend with that language, either speaking it or listening to it, we feed that spirit, we nurture it, and it strengthens." Couture spoke about how moved she was to feel the language waking up inside her body, the sensation of it being a profound experience despite her limited ability. There is a joy, there can be a joy, when speaking a simple word or a simple phrase for no other reason, no other purpose or function, than to feel its vibration in your body, to hear its sound in your voice in your own ears.

It makes me think I've had it wrong all along. That my own orienta-tion to speaking the language of my ancestors has been its own ongo-ing war, another conquest. Is there another way to be with it? Instead of acquiring it and dominating it, could I patiently tolerate an unfolding? Could I guard that tender, unformed space? Bear witness to what rises from beneath the Spanish and shows in the English we use—hammock/hamaca/jamáka, barbecue/barbacoa/barabicu, hurricane/huracán/huracan, maize/maíz/mahis—voices of the land speaking before the Spanish renamed it? Taíno. Por que dak'toká Taíno, también.

We fall apart. I fail you. You fail me. I long for you again and have to relearn the most basic words, the most elementary phrases. You refuse to become me. Will this never work out? Will we never work out? I reject you. I reject myself. I crave you again. I embarrass myself trying. I find myself resenting the white women who speak you better than I ever will. Who are praised, who have no scars from you, no lineage of baggage. Who show you off with no understanding of the pain inherent in their privilege.

Spanish.

Hispanic.

Latino/a. X.

Indígeno/a. X.

Africano/a. X.

How do you say *x* again?

My sympathetic nervous system is deployed. Fight, flight, or freeze. Wernicke's language center of the brain is put on lockdown. I am frozen.

What now? What to do with this thing, this desire, this burden, of my mother's mother tongue?

How many of us are there? Children of la isla, Borikén, in the diaspora. Where there is only English. A decoration of Spanish here and there.

Like an unkept garden in the densely overgrown brush of what has been habituated. There is what will keep growing on its own, an invasive species. Colonization of the tongue, the mouth—the feeding, the being fed, the surviving, the intimate acceptance and holding of pleasure. The naming. With this tongue, with this mouth, I speak, I hold, I force out, I take in. What is the shape of shame, or the temperature, the texture, that always accompanies it when I try to force it down? Always threatening to choke me.

In moments, there has been more ease and understanding. In most others, confusion, humiliation. The rupture is at its greatest when I try to speak the language of my Native ancestors. There I go, frozen—unable to hear, speak, or see—again.

You, Spanish, are at once familiar and forever unknown. Still, I call you in, when addressing a class of students or an audience of readers, along with the Taíno you've concealed and consumed, only to explain that I don't speak either with any real ability to communicate successfully. Rather, it's an invocation to my ancestors that they are welcome and that I acknowledge, appreciate, and include them despite the severance I often feel. Despite the oceans of time and space between us. It is my prayer of connection, of resilience, and it is heard deep inside me as the language spirit stirs.

"That 'these people' were ourselves, that this insistence on mistrust of others—that people who looked so very much like each other, who shared a common history of suffering and humiliation and enslavement, should be taught to mistrust each other, even as children, is no longer a mystery to me."

—JAMAICA KINCAID, *THE AUTOBIOGRAPHY OF MY MOTHER*

MI FAMILIA,
OR THE SPACES IN BETWEEN

I HAD KNOWN SINCE I WAS A LITTLE GIRL THAT WE HAD FAMILY in Rio Piedras. My mother's last home on the island. Because it took decades for me to visit, I had time to imagine it. Like its name, the imagining was strong, so strong that even the reality of the place when, as an adult, I stood on its streets, surrounded by its people, could not replace the imagining I'd come to claim.

Rio Piedras. River Stones. Stone River. River filled with stones.

I could see and hear the water, hold the weight of a round, smooth rock in my hand. I found myself quickly immersed in the current. Perhaps it was the river beneath the river that held my attention. "A river is a liminal place, the sacred site of in-between where magick is made. It is a place of both earth and water. Here is a divine crossroads of spiritual energy. It is fertile with potential and possibility," writes Lilith Dorsey in *Orishas, Goddesses, and Voodoo Queens*. "Oshún's river water is a divine vehicle for healing."

During a trip to the island in 2010, I went to a dance workshop in Loíza, which is in the farthest northeastern corner of Puerto Rico. Loíza, with its predominately Black population, is called "the heart of Puerto Rico's Black culture," as was explained in an article in the online magazine *Black Voice News* on April 1, 2018. It is named for its Taína cacique (chief) Yuiza, one of the first to encounter the European invaders and soon after baptized as Luisa.

Iguanas by the Rio de Loíza watched me, their eyes full of a thousand years. Full of before. The barril was made from a barrel that once held rum. Two men—one dark, one light—beat their hands against its skin. The songs were not of love and courtship, as they first seemed to be. They were songs of rebellion and reunification. Bomba. That land of swamp and shifting ground, where the river meets the sea, is holy.

I've been told this is where my great-grandparents and their parents and their parents lived and birthed and died, while the eyes of the iguanas watched. This is where I danced, where my bare feet bounced off the ground as the drum called, and the answer came, rising not only from the ground but from within me.

——

Guess.

Hawaii, Greece, Portugal, Italy, Brazil?

India, Spain, Chile, Morocco?

Argentina, Costa Rica, Turkey, Fiji, Egypt?

Iran, Syria, Tahiti, France, Lebanon?

Israel?

Are you Black? You don't look white.

Are you Native American?

It happened all the time. I was constantly interrogated in my youth. Each person asking as if they were the first and only person to question me, to make me accountable for my identity.

On this occasion, it was a steak house waitress in small-town Ohio. She asked even before bringing us water or taking our order. She was white. Everyone in the restaurant was white. My mother's third husband—or fourth, or maybe just a boyfriend—also white, sat across from me. The waitress had her order pad out, pen poised, as if my racial combination were a recipe she was going to write down, record.

"What are you?"

My mouth was pasty. I didn't know what to say. I was eleven. When I was nine, my mother had explained to my playmates' parents that we were Puerto Rican. It had been summer. I was dark enough to worry them. I stood among them as my mother named the place of our origin. I listened, too. Just like them, I needed to be educated. Just like them, I only knew Ohio.

———

Tío says, *We're Taíno.*

Tía says, *We're Black.*

But the Spanish conquered us, gave my eldest tía her light hair, made her pale but couldn't obscure features that resembled her father's.

Mami says, *We're Puerto Rican. Solamente.*

No one argues with that.

Except me. I want to use our real name.

Boricua. A word derived from the Taíno, a name not dependent on importing and exporting others' riches. Puerto Rico has long been left, like an abused wife, to beg the U.S. not to strike again with another backhanded blow. How can she ever repay the U.S.'s shady deal? She's lost so much.

Entiendo, Isla Madre, todo está muy complicado.

Yet, let us not forget her real worth. In Fajardo, on the eastern coast, you can take out a small boat at night. Pass under red mangrove trees until you reach the lagoon and there, dip your hands into the water, where you can see your skin covered in diamonds. These diamonds of light are what science calls bioluminescence.

Submerge your whole body.

The richness we hold within our skin will always belong to us. Even after the Spanish came and changed our name, even after the Americans came and turned us into property. Beauty swims within us; there is such a thing as living light. It belongs to us. Imagine, we are and have always been our own treasure.

Of the ten million enslaved Africans brought to the new, colonized world through the transatlantic slave trade between the fourteenth and seventeenth centuries, it is estimated that forty percent were shipped to the Caribbean, the other forty percent to Brazil.

In 2014, *USA Today* published an article online called "136 Variations of Brazilian Skin Colors," which begins, "When asked to describe their skin color, Brazilians came up with 136 variations." Based on a survey done in 1976 by the Brazilian Institute of Geography and Statistics and republished in a 2011 congressional document, the list "illustrates how Brazilians see themselves, a far more complex color system than simply black or white."

The catalog of skin coloring is unlike anything I'd ever heard of. I kept going back to "When asked," because the colors weren't prescribed; they weren't defined by the white-bodied powerholders and name-givers who are satisfied by the sorely inadequate reduction of white, black, brown. When the Brazilians answered for themselves, there was no shortage of terms. Definitions flourished in variety and lush specificity. Nearly twelve dozen ways to see oneself and to see each other, to be seen.

> Acastanhada: Somewhat chestnut-colored. Agalegada: Somewhat like a Galician. Alva: Snowy white. Alva escura: Dark snowy white. Alvarenta (not in dictionary; poss. dialect): Snowy white. Alvarinta: Snowy white. Alva rosada: Pinkish white. Alvinha: Snowy white. Amarela: Yellow. Amarelada: Yellowish. Amarela-queimada: Burnt yellow. Amarelosa: Yellowy. Amorenada: Somewhat dark-skinned. Avermelhada: Reddish. Azul: Blue. Azul-marinho: Sea blue.

For my mother, who for the majority of her life on the mainland was separated from her family and any Puerto Rican community, there seemed to be a clear directive: to pass. In the racially charged 1960s (is there ever a time in U.S. history that can't be described as "racially charged"?), I imagine it did not take much for her to understand the violent border between Black and white in this country. She spent years secluded in a Catholic orphanage on Staten Island—a place she always referred to as "the mission," where she was punished for speaking Spanish—followed by brief stints with various older siblings before enlisting in the United States Army and meeting the man who would become my father. In those formative years, her identity was influenced by those around her telling her who she should be—there was the island colorism replicated and apparent in her own family, who were favored because they were lighter in skin, lighter in hair, lighter in eye color; and there was the racism of the country she also belonged to, offering her better opportunities with its institutions—religious and military—that took nearly anyone but did not treat them equally.

As a Boricua stripped of her language and culture, she seemed to feel most comfortable and safe hiding behind "exotic."

Exotic.

Add beautiful.

Add nice.

And you have an aesthetically pleasing, nonthreatening woman of questionable origin. Few were familiar with Puerto Rico across the small rural towns in central Ohio where she migrated. Being light-skinned and speaking without an accent provided a thin margin of acceptance. She was on occasion permitted access: to rent a chair at a barbershop, to obtain a car loan, to secure housing in a region dominated by white body supremacy. That she cut the hair of the husbands and sons at the all-white church she attended meant there was a certain amount of leash, of permission she was given with minimal questioning.

But not so much permission that she might use it to trust herself, use that trust to imagine something, anything, better. More whole. I was her understudy growing up. Comprehending that how I looked made others uneasy or confused also, somehow, made it my responsibility to calm them, to list my genetic ingredients. The trained smile. The trained responsibility of taking care, of providing an answer, again and again, to the question, "What are you?"

In the pause before I could respond, I often heard the same thing, as if to excuse or hide the inherent racist undertone:

"I mean, you're so exotic. Beautiful."

———

I hold the memory close as if it were this:

"Ma, where did you get your shoulders from?"

She stands on a dock beside the small pond in her front yard. We've lived in eight different towns in seventeen years, a new apartment each year, sometimes a small house, always in a perpetual state of packing and unpacking. Now she has found a permanent home in rural northeastern Ohio—forty acres, horses, woods, two ponds, and a husband to grow old with. We are both in swimsuits. Hers is maroon and pulls across her round abdomen and full hips. She has made a great effort to keep her hair dry.

"What kind of question is that? That's just the way I was made." Her shoulders and upper arms are tight bundles of muscle. "It's all those years I cut hair." Her eyes fight the reflection on the water. I can't tell if she can see anything through her squint. "Maybe it's because I'm a good swimmer."

"But Ma, my shoulders look just like yours," I say. "And I've never cut hair and I hate to swim." I stamp my wet feet on the sun-bleached dock, making a pattern with my heels. "I can't even swim, really."

"Ah, yes, mi'jita. You have shoulders like mine." Pride fills her voice.

"So, where did you get yours from?" I try again.

Silence. She closes her eyes. Now that she's no longer squinting, her face is soft, unlined.

I've caught her. She has always made me an extension of her, but she won't acknowledge any lineage beyond her. She won't admit that her logic does not work.

"I just have them, that's all," she says defiantly, and turns away from me to face the sun.

Tío, is it true that in Rio Piedras none of you wore clothes? I imagine the sticks and stones of your bodies in that crowded landscape—moss foaming over roofs, wild green cracking open concrete, bush and tree and flowering vine a constant force even in the suburb of San Juan where you all lived. Mami told me you had to dig through trash on the streets to find something to eat. You did not have a pair of shoes, a shirt, anything to protect even your most private of parts? Mami says she looked like the photos cataloged in the archives documenting island poverty—children with distended bellies, naked, dirty, feral. I can see the stones of your small knees and hips, your round heads heavy like melons.

Did you ever hear our creation story? No one I asked could tell it to me. I had to hunt it down on the internet. One version begins with two brothers fighting on top of a mountain. A mountain smothered by forest. It was so tall, the clouds nested in its peak. One brother dropped the calabaza he was carrying. It tumbled down the mountain, rupturing, and do you know what came out? The contents of the entire sea, the water and the animales del mar, all poured out, surrounding the mountain on all sides, creating la isla, Borikén. From the inside of that calabaza we emerged; from the sea came our ancestors. We are nothing but pulp and wet seeds, raw and pungent with life.

Were you all really that poor? Did you climb the red mangrove trees and hunt those tiny yellow birds with your handmade slingshots? So little meat, so many bones. Did you eat the bones, too, after you roasted, blackened over a fire, those little beasts of the air? I imagine the mosquitoes swarming, a hide covering your skin—after all, no one would have been there to show you how to put coca husks over the flames to keep them away. You, squatting while clenching the skewered fists of feathers, devouring even the head and crisp claws. Your teeth sharp in their scavenging. Your teeth. Even your teeth ached with hunger.

Did the girls hunt, too? The youngest tía was too little, but the eldest tía and even my mami, they were climbing those trees, too, weren't they? With worms infesting their bellies and their feet, tightly coiled hair so long it threatened to overtake their torsos.

The tías say it's all nonsense. That none of it is true.

"Cállate," one tía says to me. "Nobody ate any birds."

What did those birds taste like, when they were dead and fit into the palm of your child-sized hand? Did they sing before you felled them from the trees? After you had eaten them, could you hear their song rising from deep within you?

"Cállate, already."

But there are too many rumors. My unanswered questions take the lead, dragging me along.

The eldest tía went blind in one eye before your papi rescued all of you and delivered you to the father you would always have and obey, Papi America.

Papi Nueva York.

Papi Brooklyn.

Then, later, for each of you someplace different—

Papi Minnesota.

Papi Iowa.

Papi Texas.

Papi New Jersey.

Papi Alabama.

Papi Ohio.

It seems you all tried as adults to mend the tears that separated you, to bind yourselves together again, but for my mother—and us, her daughters—the connection remained frayed, continuously unraveling. I wonder if my mother thought that by scattering, remaining loosely connected, she could shed the misaligned shame she'd internalized, a shame that belonged to those who'd benefited from colonization and capitalism. What other memories were there besides eating birds, being naked in the streets, climbing through trash in the dense humid air, your stomachs showing signs of kwashiorkor?

In the 1950s, the U.S. sought to control Puerto Rican women's bodies, their fertility. Many were forcibly sterilized without their knowledge or consent, while others were used as test subjects for what would become the pill, without being given a thorough explanation of the harm it could cause at that early phase in its development. At the same time, on the West Side of NYC, the majority Puerto Rican neighborhood of San Juan Hill was deemed "the worst slum in the city" by the New York Housing Authority, and plans to level it began. In 1958, the New York Giants lost the world championship, Alaska became a state, and Elvis Presley joined the army. All this while the Statue of Liberty held her lamp to guide you. Did you feel so very small in the city that would become your home for the rest of your life? Did anyone spit on you? Call you a spic? (The word it derives from, Hispanic, *also always sounds like a slur to my ears.) How soon before you realized that all you'd carried with you to America was shame?*

Mami had diphtheria, right? Almost died. What happened to you? Did you ever get sick? Mami says, "Don't tell. This stays in the family." She cut the cloth of our family to fit only her and us, her three daughters. I am the baby. Tío, did anyone even call you to announce that I had been born? On the same day as your father's birthday, May 10. How long before you knew I existed? Mami squeezed us into the boat of her body, into her arms, and we drifted far—far away from Rio Piedras, from San Juan, from Loíza, far from Papi Nueva York. Far away from all of you, away from anything that would have reminded us of who we were.

"Don't tell," she says. But I have to.

Baiano: From Bahia. Bem branca: Very white. Bem clara: Very pale. Bem morena: Very dark-skinned. Branca: White. Branca-avermelhada: White going on for red. Branca-melada: Honey-colored white. Branca-morena: White but dark-skinned. Branca-palida: Pale white. Branca-queimada: Burnt white. Branca-sardenta: Freckled white. Branca-suja: Off-white. Branquica: Whitish. Branquinha: Very white. Bronze: Bronze-colored. Bronzeada: Sun-tanned. Bugrezinha-escura: Dark-skinned India. Burro-quando-foge: Disappearing donkey (i.e., nondescript) *humorous.*

————

The woman in the advertisement hides behind a giant green leaf. A hole in the foliage reveals her right eye and eyebrow, barely visible. Most of her flat stomach is visible, her narrow waist, the wink of her belly button. Half of her crotch, covered by black scalloped panties—or a bikini bottom, hard to say—is visible. She wears an oversized pink button-down dress shirt, closed at the wrists but open in the front. It's wet at the bottom and along the arm where she holds the leaf she's hiding behind. Her legs are separated, open, her left hip jutting out in typical model stance.

"Get lost and see what you find. LIVE Boricua. Discover Puerto Rico," the caption reads in a tourism advertisement for the island. Her skin is a shade of rose similar to that of the shirt she wears. The flora and fauna of the background are blurred. "No passport required for U.S. citizens," reads a faux white stamp in the corner of the page. A definition of "Boricua" lines the bottom in small lettering: "Boricua [boh-ree-kwah] is more than a word to identify a person from Puerto Rico. It's a way of life that finds joy and beauty in the unexpected. So let yourself wander our island and discover amazing places around every corner. Book your trip today." The advertisement ran in *The New York Times Magazine* in the summer of 2022. Despite the pandemic, desperation and exploitation converged—Puerto Rico still needed tourism to survive, and property sales spiked.

I wonder about the marketing team deciding on images—something with broad appeal (to privileged tourists), which looks nonthreatening (to privileged tourists), with models whose body language says, "Bienvenidos." Tourism and gentrification the modern, most recognizable forms of ongoing colonization.

And who defined "Boricua"? Willing to sell even our original name, as if it were accessible to anyone.

———

The young women that surrounded me in public school became my ideal. Built like prepubescent boys, with thin hair, thin lips, and webs of veins pulsing beneath pale skin, they embodied a standard of beauty, an unattainable purity.

Let me make my voice higher. See? Nothing to be afraid of. I have no

*power; I've given it all to you. I can be nicer. I can try to hide from the sun.
I can pretend not to hear you when you ask me where I'm from.*

These were the descendants of English, French, German, Irish, and Dutch immigrants. Young women who farmed after school and were crowned homecoming queen, who went to the county fair and to farm auctions with their fathers, drove miles to the closest city with their mothers on Saturdays to shop at the mall. These were the young women who surrounded me in my youth while I developed and bled each month—who were surely experiencing their own growing pains and high school torment that, in my own isolation and vulnerability, I could not see. I was busy hiding from myself and idolizing them. My full mouth smeared with tacky lip gloss while I lay on the floor of the high school library reading *YM, Sassy,* and *Mademoiselle* magazines, plotting how to become just like those young women as I flipped through image after image of pale and light, beautiful and pure. The ideal was clear, the repetition a tool that further diminished my appearance. Because I could not see myself and there was no one else like me—with the exception of my mother—I couldn't fully identify myself. No matter where I looked, the images did not reflect me. My mother and I were the only ones foolish enough to believe the lie that she perpetuated: that we even had a chance of passing.

My mother was exasperated by my temporary shameful lapses. The way I would veer from the status quo from time to time, flirt with showcasing my status as "other."

"Take that scarf out of your hair. Do you know what you look like? Take that piercing out of your nose. Wipe that eye makeup off. Remember to always say *please* and *thank you*. Remember to always ask permission—not *can I, may I*. Do you really want to wear your hair in two braids like that? Show some class."

Forgive them, I was instructed, even when names—squaw and nigger and spic and cunt—swarmed and stung.

"Don't draw any more attention to yourself. You already stand out enough."

My mother would tell me this while her nipples—visible through her thinning bra—were aimed at me from beneath her satin blouse. She was a neon sign of fetishized beauty in her tight slacks and high heels, lips consumed by fuchsia, whips of hot-rolled long black hair. I would challenge her litany with one look, my left eyebrow raised, the corner of my mouth smirking.

"Do as I say, not as I do," she told me, and even with this flimsy reasoning, I was convinced she knew best. Her hand would strike if I pushed any further. A slap across the face or the back of the head would always silence my rage, sending it deeper, where it would smolder.

Let me try again. I'll wear more beige and nothing that shows cleavage. I won't paint my lips red. That only makes them bigger. I'll hide my ass. I'll try not to eat so much. Wear makeup that makes my skin appear lighter. I can hardly eat anything at all. I can try to look like a twelve-year-old boy.

I was familiar with my classmates' homes, where the mantels were like altars, cluttered with family photos, evidence of all the generations that had come before. I never saw a picture of my mother as a child, her family in Puerto Rico. There was no evidence of who had come before. Our living room featured framed art found at an antiques store, bookshelves full of fake plants, fake fruit, and a few archaic books that were used as decoration. The only photo on display was one taken of my mother, my sisters, and me when I was around four years old. It was in those classmates' living rooms where, sitting in front of the TV eating cookies and chips, they would turn and say, unprompted and with an air of love and loyalty, "You're not any color. You're just my friend," and I would feel temporarily absolved from the sin of my skin, the skin that proved I was unlike them, no matter how hard I tried to pretend otherwise.

I'm sorry. Let me try again. To look like you so you will see me. If I try hard enough, maybe I can disappear. Disappear into you. Disappear into the wooden pews of your church; disappear behind all God's children who eat chicken nuggets, mashed potatoes, and creamed corn; disappear into overalls and Carhartt jackets; disappear into clapboard houses and red barns; disappear into American-made cars and small-town parades; dis-

appear in sitcoms, on billboards, in movies, in magazine advertisements; disappear in the history books, where—see?—I don't even exist.

Cabocla: Copper-colored (refers to Indians). Cabo-verde: From Cabo Verde (Cape Verde). Cafe: Coffee-colored. Cafe-com-leite: Cafe au lait. Canela: Cinnamon. Canelada: Somewhat like cinnamon. Cardao: Color of the cardoon, or thistle (blue-violet). Castanha: Chestnut. Castanha-clara: Light chestnut. Castanha-escura: Dark chestnut. Chocolate: Chocolate-colored. Clara: Light-colored, pale. Clarinha: Light-colored, pale. Cobre: Copper-colored. Corada: With a high color. Cor-de-cafe: Coffee-colored. Cor-de-canela: Cinnamon-colored. Cor-de-cuia: Gourd-colored. Cor-de-leite: Milk-colored (i.e., milk-white). Cor-de-ouro: Gold-colored (i.e., golden). Cor-de-rosa: Pink. Cor-firme: Steady-colored. Crioula: Creole.

All my mother remembers of Aniceto's mother, my great-grandmother, was that she sat in a wheelchair, having suffered physical limitations from a stroke. But the tales I heard were of the wealth of love she gave to her grandchildren despite her own suffering and restriction. I've often wondered why my mother didn't want to be more like her, given that she was always the one who remained faultless in my mother's island memories, a familial icon of love. That my mother didn't remember her grandmother's strength and want to associate herself with her or claim her identity as the descendant of her dark-skinned abuela, her Black father, continues to cause me sadness. Could my mother not see herself either?

In my formative years, she never claimed her Afro-Taíno family. And if mother-daughter relationships can be a form of call-and-response, I've lived my life contrary to hers. I can't claim what is not my experience. Sidelining the white component in my mixed racial heritage, I've focused instead on what has systematically been devalued and ignored,

vilified. I like to think I would have done this regardless of my appearance. But I will say this: Being set apart, questioned, made to answer for
my appearance, mostly to white people, thousands of times in my life,
has compelled me to include my darker family—grandparents, aunts,
uncles, cousins, second cousins—and thereby include myself.

"Not white enough, not Black enough," my mother shared in her
later years, well after turning seventy. A lifetime of skirting the edges of a
Black experience and a white experience, not fully claimed by either one.
Only then did she claim the complexity and toxicity of colorism within
her own family, her confusion over how to experience herself and her
negligence in providing me with any anchoring for my own experiences
with race and racism. She left me exposed and confused, while I fought
myself and everyone else who told me what they saw when they looked
at me.

——

Regardless of how my mother rejected her own color, and the darker
ones of our family—decades later, she says it's because they rejected
her—she was the only person I could reference growing up in an expanse
of whiteness that made sure to single me out, set me apart. During my
formative years, she was the only one from whom I could garner any
sense of who I was, whom I came from. If I couldn't see myself, did I
even exist? Wounded and troubled as she was, my mother is my origin
story, and for a long time, she was my only access to the island, to my
extended family.

——

*Tía, is it true that, in Puerto Rico, you experienced material wealth before
the poverty? Mami says she can almost remember your parents, Aida and
Aniceto, when they were still married. Was there a hacienda with hired
help and an elevator in the kitchen? Do you remember wearing a velvet
dress? Tell me how it felt against your knees as you ran through the yard,
welcoming the friends of your parents, while the coquí cried,* Darkness is
coming. *Did your mother with her proper Spanish upbringing make ring-*

lets with your hair, fasten gold ribbons to the ends? She was olive-skinned with fine red hair, and her husband was dark. You, the eldest daughter, were the lightest one. Is that why she favored you?

What did you see before your eye confused itself with blindness? Were you downstairs while the party lit the house with music and loose hips, lit the trees in the yard, their limbs weighted with ripe fruit? Did you know your mother loved another man? That she managed to steal moments to touch her tongue to his when she wasn't listening to soap operas on the radio and naming her daughters after the actresses? Tía, did you know that twenty-eight years after my mami was named, she was naming me after a character, too? Jaime Sommers from The Bionic Woman, *whom she perhaps hoped I would grow up to emulate. Someone who possessed extraordinary strength and supernatural gifts.*

This is how I imagine it. Cigarette smoke. Rum on breath. Damp brows and breasts and the fashionable flared skirts from the 1950s sewn from American patterns. The humidity saturating every porous surface. The dark hand of your father as he grabbed a knife from the kitchen after seeing his wife disappear into the mouth of another man. The blood darker as it colored the other man's undershirt, his dress shirt, his linen suit jacket.

Do you ever wonder if your mother wished it had been her, instead? That she had been the one your father killed, released from her body instead of forced to live with ten children all shades of blanco y negro and a husband who no longer loved her? Or was this just a story you remember from listening to soap operas on the radio? Was it that night that he left for America and took your mother with him? Is that why he never went back? Even when you could no longer see out of your eye?

You all say that he sent money. You all say that he cared, that he loved each of you, even when he remarried and his new wife birthed more children. All this while you were forced to bury your face in the trash, asking, Is there anything to eat in here?

Is that how your eye got sick? From something rotten trying to hide in your eye? Mami says he sent money to his sister, who was supposed to be taking care of all ten of you. How many children of her own did she have?

There was a hole in the middle of the bed. Ten children, one bed. When I asked my mother about what it was like to live in Puerto Rico, this was what she would tell me. "The hole was this big," she'd say, holding her hands apart to imply the size of a basketball. Then, remembering more accurately her personal relationship with the hole, she'd increase the space between her hands and correct herself: "No, actually, it was twice that size."

How did you fit? At night, on the bed with no sheets and a hole in the middle? With no spaces between you and your siblings, like cargo on a little mattress ship, with no one to save you and feed you and keep you safe?

I try to imagine whose toes tapped whose head, whose arm covered whose neck, who told the stories, who fell asleep first, who had to sleep closest to the hole, who fell through.

Naked, I stand in front of the mirror. I try not to be afraid. I try to see myself. I'm not alone. A crowd of ancestors gather. They point to my small lobed ears, my chin, my narrow ankles, the high arches of my feet, the perfectly round black mole above my navel—note my willfulness in claiming them, my stubborn attempts to be inclusive.

From Borikén to San Juan Bautista to Puerto Rico to Porto Rico and back again to Puerto Rico, it is apparent what a striated and complex place the island is in the history of the name changes alone. Or in the octopi of Puerto Rican politics—statehood, autonomy, or independence. Or in the informal economy and the geography of consumption, or the majority of census reports that indicate a white population of close to ninety percent. This is in direct opposition to the findings of geneticist Dr. Juan Carlos Martínez-Cruzado in the early 2000s, when island-wide genetic testing revealed that sixty-one percent of the population is Native, twenty-seven percent of African descent, and twelve percent Caucasian.

Given all these positions, these arguments, what are we supposed to believe? What does it mean to be Puerto Rican? What does it look like?

When the United States began its efforts to "Americanize" the island after acquiring it in 1898, thus introducing another wave of colonization and occupation, the complexities became pressurized. In 2019—more than a century after Puerto Ricans gained citizenship in 1917—five million Puerto Ricans lived off island, while just over three million remained. By the year 2050, there will be more elders on the island than young people and, due to rising sea levels caused by global warming, less available land—yet another combination of factors to add to the precarious mix of identity, place, and belonging.

Some islanders and those in the diaspora, including my own family, seem to lean heavily on their Spanish heritage. "Dress like a señorita," my mother would tell me, steering me away from my tendency to reach for complex and bold tribal expressions that would signal that I wasn't a lady.

Encerada: Polished. Enxofrada: Pallid. Esbranquecimento: Whitening. Escura: Dark. Escurinha: Very dark. Fogoio: Having fiery-colored hair. Galega: Galician or Portuguese. Galegada: Somewhat like a Galician or Portuguese. Jambo: Light-skinned (the color of a type of apple). Laranja: Orange. Lilas: Lilac. Loira: Blonde. Loira-clara: Light blonde. Loura: Blonde. Lourinha: Petite blonde.

———

My mother sits at the kitchen table with her sisters. I'm twenty-four years old, and this is the first time I've met the youngest sister, who hosts us, or the eldest sister, both my tías. The eldest is the authority on memories from la isla.

"I remember this one time one of you was upstairs in front of the window," she begins.

I watch my mother try to lower herself in her chair. She pulls up the hanging tablecloth and tries to cover herself with it. The shaking from her laughter not only consumes her body but also vibrates across the table, making the gardenias in the centerpiece tremble and disturbing the water in my glass.

The story continues.

"One of you saw us kids down below, passing by, and got our attention by sticking her bare butt out the window. But not only did she show us her bare butt—"

At that, my three tías twist and contort with fits of deep laughter as their eldest sister recounts the event. The labor of laughter causes her to break out in a sweat. Small points of perspiration dot her forehead and upper lip. She fans herself with an insert from the newspaper and, after a moment, continues.

"Not only did she show us her bare butt, she opened her cheeks to us, airing out her dirty crack. And one of the kids, never mind who it was, I can't remember, said, 'Ábrelo más!' "

I'm lost until my mother, through her hysterical laughter, translates for me.

"And she did. One of you pulled her cheeks farther apart. 'Wider!' they screamed, jumping up and down in the road cheering her on, and she did, she did open it wider!"

More howling from all of them. My tía pauses in her narration, fans herself vigorously. "In fact, your mother," she finally says to me, her voice becoming hoarse, "pulled and pulled so hard that we were placing bets on how soon it would be before she split herself in two."

"That was not me," my mother objected, with mock indignance, once she had recovered from her laughter and could speak again.

"You were wild!"

"So were you!" my mother screamed at her sister.

Another wave of howling ensued.

I wanted to do more than chuckle now and then as the story unfolded, but I couldn't. I tried to reconcile this new information I had about my mother, but I couldn't. At what point did the fierceness give way to the paper doll I knew—obedient and dominated, bent and arranged into any position that suited whatever man was in charge? What were the other stories that would tell me who my mother once was, who my family was, and, therefore, who I am? What were the stories that came before the apologizing and shame? A mix of emotions flared within me.

Imagining my mother's ass hanging out the window as she spread her cheeks for all to see was less about the actual act and more about the symbolism. Here was my mother, unruly, audacious, and innocent. Here was a force of spiritedness that was the opposite of assimilation. In her behavior, I could see even more clearly what was stolen from her, that which had to hide while she performed a different self.

The sisters sobered up. My mother shook her head. She didn't remember. She swore she didn't remember. She remembered having tapeworms and screaming on the toilet and no one coming to help her while they tickled her bobo. I knew that story. That story got told along with the hole-in-the-bed story. When my mother told me about Puerto Rico, what I heard was "It was dirty. We were poor and, some of us, very dark."

———

In my twenties, when people asked me what I was or where I was from, I began to tell them that my family—my mother's family—was from Puerto Rico. This often inspired the next question. "Have you been?" And when I answered no, I had not, and added that my mother had not been back either, not since she left as a girl, the questioner would often appear disturbed.

Their face creased in perplexity. Their eyes narrowed in judgment. I would stop the volley of question and answer at this point.

I would not tell them what my mother told me, that Puerto Rico was a dirty place, that we were dirty, and that behind the façade of downtown San Juan, the private beaches and gated communities—and the few blocks that protect the tourists, who descend from gleaming cruise ships as if descending from the heavens—is the rest of the island, the real territory, that is to be feared and guarded against even by the very children the island bore.

Sitting at that dining room table with the strangers who were my blood—my mother's sisters—I did not yet know about the Taíno women of the island. I did not yet know with any kind of specificity about the African women—from Nigeria, Ghana, Tongo, Benin, Cameroon, and Congo—who were forced to lay bricks in the streets of San Juan, bricks taken from the ballast of the very ships they had been chained and stored in. I did not know that those women were my ancestors and that my body was the rightful territory they inhabited.

This was the first and only time I had been with all of my tías and my mother, a precious event that is commonplace to most. The way their laughter sounded the same, the way they were different but echoed each other with varying accents, was overwhelming. Like soil during the first rain after a drought, I could not absorb it fully, hold on to it. It seemed to still be an experience I wasn't having but rather longed to have.

For a few minutes, it was quiet at the table. My mother examined her empty coffee cup. My aunt cleared her throat while she picked at her cuticles, the aftermath of laughter still illuminating their faces.

———

A year after I went to Puerto Rico for the first time, Justice Sonia Sotomayor visited the Institute of American Indian Arts, where I was attending college. I was taken with her height, her broad shoulders, the power of her physicality and stature, her accomplishments, her smile as she asked me where on the island my family was from.

She had asked me first in Spanish.

Overcome by her presence, as someone who shared my lineage in the highest position in the U.S. justice system, I froze. There was so much I wanted to tell her, that I wanted to ask, *to know,* that I could not form one single word in Spanish or in English.

She asked me again, slower and in English, and my nervousness dissipated through an awkward fit of laughter.

Gracefully, she chuckled along with me.

"Loíza," I told her. "Carolina and Rio Piedras."

Justice Sotomayor had just spoken to my peers, who, at this tribal arts college, were mainly Native people from nearly a hundred different tribal nations across the U.S. mainland, Hawaii, and Alaska. I had felt more comfortable, more whole, at this institution of higher learning, among this community, than at any other I'd tried as an undergraduate transferring from one university to another over the span of four-teen years, attempting to find a place where I could learn and grow with the totality of myself and my ancestry. A place to be mentored in the flourishing of my creativity and imagination, while not being further erased and further constructed in an image of the academic institution, stripped of the culture and identity I so desperately needed and wanted to repair after my mother's rupture of assimilation. Where education was not wielded as a tool of cultural genocide but was, and is, in service of reclamation, inclusion, preservation, and promotion of one's culture and identity. For those of us who had been silenced, erased, and mar-ginalized, IAIA was an institution that advanced our education while giving us the gift of ourselves, activating creativity that included our ancestors' presence; our homelands; a multitude of intelligences, lan-guages, and knowledge systems; and our communities. All essential to learning.

Along with Howard and Gallaudet Universities, the Institute of American Indian Arts is a federally funded institution, a line item in the budget, affected by who has been voted into power. Sotomayor had spent the previous days visiting Pueblo, invited by her friend and former Princeton University classmate Regis Pecos, previously the governor of Cochiti Pueblo.

Before I introduced myself to Justice Sotomayor, shook her hand, and moused my way through my responses to her questions, I had heard her speak to the complexity of our identity, claiming all its parts as I was intent on also doing despite the impatience and ignorance often present in the listener. I doubt that she wore her robe, but that's how I picture her in my memory, as an authority. A Boricua woman who was found worthy of being sworn into the highest court in the U.S. despite back-lash against a comment she made when she was nominated in August 2009 by President Obama, that a "wise Latina" might reach a better decision than a white man.

Yes, this authority, her audacity.

How dare she speak truth to power? Be chosen, be included in dis-seminating that power through protecting the rule of law?

Only the third woman to be nominated to the Supreme Court in U.S. history, and the first Latina—her confirmation was groundbreaking. It continues to fill me with pride, even while I simultaneously criticize the U.S. government's policies and acts of domination, of ongoing colonization on the island. But there was that moment, my hand in hers as we shook hello, all the internal and external miles she'd traveled in her lifetime to sit in that position. Another Boricua woman I could look to as an affirmation of worth, of dignity. The right to be heard, the need to be heard, to hear myself and act as my own authority. This woman, only a handful of years younger than my mother, provided a necessary and alternative example.

Eight years after I shook Justice Sotomayor's hand, Alexandria Ocasio-Cortez, known as AOC, was elected to the U.S. Congress and became a representative for New York's 14th Congressional District. Of a younger generation than Sotomayor or myself, she is another example and inspiration. Beyond her social media feeds of her cooking and chatting, or her iconic red lipstick, I would note the conviction she held for her own identity as a Boricua woman who consistently supported anti-racist and anti-classist policies while sustaining her courage in the face of the negativity aimed at her, threats against her safety and her life. Still, she maintained the power of her voice in calling us to bring ourselves forward fully and imagine our shared reality differently, better.

These, too, are the women I come from, our homeland held in kinship. Boricuas en la luna. How do they alter the stories I tell? How do their examples magnify what is right and what is wrong? How do I hold their experiences and my experience simultaneously—the similarities, the differences? I hold them and reach past them toward Borikén, the island it is now. My reach continues farther across space and time, bodies, wombs, and centuries.

Malaia: Malaysian woman. Marinheira: Sailor-woman. Marrom: Brown. Meio-amarela: Half-yellow. Meio-branca: Half-white. Meio-morena: Half dark-skinned. Meio-preta: Half-black. Melada: Honey-colored. Mestica: Half-caste/mestiza. Miscigenacao: Miscegenation. Mista: Mixed. Morena: Dark-skinned, brunette. Morena-bem-chegada: Very nearly morena. Morena-bronzeada: Sunburnt morena. Morena-canelada: Somewhat cinnamon-colored morena. Morena-castanha: Chestnut-colored morena. Morena-clara: Light-skinned morena. Morena-cor-de-canela: Cinnamon-colored morena. Morena-jambo: Light-skinned morena. Morenada: Somewhat morena. Morena-escura: Dark morena. Morena-fechada: Dark morena. Morenao: Dark-complexioned man. Morena-parda: Dark morena. Morena-roxa: Purplish morena. Morena-ruiva: Red-headed morena. Morena-trigueira: Swarthy, dusky morena. Moreninha: Petite morena. Mulata: Mulatto girl. Mulatinha: Little mulatto girl.

———

It seems as if everyone around me is talking about where they come from, their people. Or am I imagining it? In Santa Fe, there are conversations seemingly everywhere—in galleries, in cafés, on the streets among people walking their dogs. Pairs and small crowds, explaining where they come from, a land beyond their mother's womb. I overhear them and consider my own possibilities. Again, I return to my mother's body as my origin story, the island of her.

———

A conch shell, a clamshell, an oyster shell, wombs like watery melons, fat and ripe, stitched with seams of green, blue, and purple veins. An extension cord, an umbilical cord, a rope hanging from a tree, from an anchor, a belt, a braid, a strand of hair.

———

In Museo Castillo Serrallés, home of the Don Juan Serrallés rum empire that spanned from the late nineteenth century through three subsequent generations in Ponce, what haunted me were the places I didn't see.

I saw images taken in the 1920s. Portraits of creased brown faces staring at the camera with eyes that spoke of hard labor and exhaustion,

dressed in ragged clothes and standing in front of the tiny wooden closets they called housing. The gulf between the Serrallés family—with
excesses of wealth from sugar and rum profits—and the laborers whose
backs the sugar was carried on. From the fields of sugarcane came sugar;
from sugar came molasses and rum. All key ingredients for their gold, or
rather, Serrallés Don Q Cristal.

I saw two mannequins in maid apparel, glaringly white and six feet
tall, with obscene eyelashes that rimmed their painted glass eyes. One
in the dining room, one in the kitchen. I saw the two-foot-tall pestle
used to grind coffee and the three circular slabs of rock with a hole in
the center used to grind corn. The ceiba tree and the dormilón tree in
the yard, matriarchs. I tried to guess how old they were—three, four,
five hundred years old? Massive beings of roots and branches anchored
in the ground, not unlike the laborers who wore the filth and fertility of
the earth on their skin.

What I didn't see was the basement where the servants stayed.

In the town of Ponce, on a walking tour ten years before the earthquakes that began in 2019, I learned that Nuestra Señora de Guadalupe,
for whom the church on the plaza is named, was adopted by the people
as their own. And that a separate statue depicts three different images of
women—one of motherhood, one of the woman of the future, and one
of the workingwoman. They all sit on triangular bases, the triangle being
a significant shape in Taíno symbolism, representing the womb. As the
tour was completed, I passed a five- or six-year-old boy feeding his sandwich to a flock of pigeons. There were easily forty or more around him,
and he was sitting on the sidewalk with his head back, laughing with his
entire body.

While I was in La Guancha, pelicans behaved as if they were pigeons,
strutting about the boardwalk next to people, waiting to be fed. I ate
filete de chillo, badly, as I never maneuver well around anything with
bones, but I was in La Guancha, and I tried. After eating, I visited a vendor's stand and picked out a five-dollar necklace. An elongated triangle
hanging from a leather cord. Between my awkward Spanish and the
artist's awkward English, I understood that the pendant was made from

bone, from a sea animal, but which one, I'll never know. The artist and I shook our heads at each other—seeing ourselves mirrored but unable to comprehend. Music vibrated from giant speakers as a group of young men danced with a woman who must have been in her late nineties. She shuffled and bobbed, her hands in the air, while chewing on her gums. She was in her Sunday best: a pastel suit and a floral blouse.

Museo Serrallés continues to haunt me—how priceless common people and common events endure, despite all that is lost, so much sweeter and more satisfying than the empire's seduction.

———

In the spring of 2022, the former mayor of San Juan, Carmen Yulín Cruz Soto, spoke on the podcast *Our Body Politic* about being a leader in practice. While opinions of her overall term of service vary, I was invested in what she had to say. In the wake of Hurricane Maria, Cruz spoke to the layers of devastation, of an island dramatically changed.

Over three thousand lives lost.

Thirty million trees lost.

All are noted and grieved.

What might have been hidden from some could no longer be ignored, the neglect that killed Puerto Rican people, Boricuas, the abandonment of the island that is still a possession of the U.S. Cared for like an object, a thing, but not respected, not included, not equal.

"We're people of color, we are a colony. . . . Our lives were expendable." Because of racism, she explained, "People . . . let others die because of who they were."

For nearly the past two decades, public distrust of the government has been growing on the island. Most recently, the private contracts for utilities have left islanders with a rise in bills they struggle to afford while being regularly left in the dark, without power. "Every day, it's harder to live on the island. Every day, it's harder to access resources for islanders," says freelance journalist Bianca Graulau in Bad Bunny's docu-music video, "El Apagón—Aquí Vive Gente," released in the fall of 2022.

In the video, Boricuas speak to the impact tax incentives for foreigners, like Act 22 and Act 60, have on their daily lives. With zero percent capital gains tax and the low property costs after Hurricane Maria, as one Boricua puts it, "Puerto Rico is on a silver platter." Graulau references history, the U.S. takeover in the nineteenth century, which oversaw "the sugar plantations that kept workers and exploited them, a practice that continues today," and juxtaposes this with the wealthy land vultures moving in to make a profit in Puerto Rico, their monies funneled to politicians who will in turn secure their interests.

The island stands in perilous danger. The consequences of this new face of colonization—gentrification and tourism—are the same as those of its predecessor.

What Mami cannot describe to me:

The sound of a mango as it falls against the roof, tumbles to the ground at dawn. *There are a thousand different kinds.* How tall her grandfather was, how high the lift into his arms. How many braids were in her grandmother's hair. The color of orchids, *a hundred thousand different kinds,* their roots in the air in El Yunque. The taste of sugarcane, fibrous strands, stubborn as forgetting, stuck between her teeth. The hands bound to its harvest. *A hundred trillion cells, a whole body, flooded with longing.*

Fifty miles from the northern shore of Puerto Rico, two tectonic plates continue to slide against each other. One hundred and fifty-three million years ago, the North American and Caribbean plates began an argument, a passionate dance, a grieving, perhaps, that created the island of Borikén. Because of this continued friction, a tremendous amount of seismic activity produces waves of concentrated energy, resulting in mini earthquakes every day, moments of the land shuddering or trembling. This is information presented by the scientific world, which measures, counts, and collects data, provides the world with facts. However, I can't help but remember the capacity we all have as human beings to create a story that goes beyond the reason of science, feeding the ancient hunger of the spirit.

Perhaps Puerto Rico is trying to shake the rain from her lush coat like a perro throwing off water in a full-body shake after swimming or having been subjected to a bath. After all, the average annual rainfall on the island is seventy inches. In El Yunque, it's over two hundred inches per year. Or perhaps El Yunque is a deity with a story of his own. Tries to keep peace between his beloved island—with all her voluptuous curves of green and the inhabitants who decorate her hills with their colorful casas—and the deities, our ancestors at the bottom of the sea, the second-deepest waters on the planet at nearly seven and a half miles. Multiple times a day, he makes this journey from the top of the rainforest to the bottom of the sea, and those who are sensitive to the energies of the natural world, who have open hearts, who believe in the supernatural, can feel it.

I can feel it.

Meanwhile, Puerto Rico has been trying to keep pace with urban sprawl and consumer economies. Fourteen Kmarts, 17 Walmarts, 161 shopping centers, and 5.8 pounds of garbage per person per day—and my stats are a decade old. Does an island that is among the world's largest in population density at 1,100 people per square mile (more densely populated than any of the 50 states) have the room to submit to this kind of consumption? If it keeps up this pace, will there be enough room for all the people and the things they purchased? Will Puerto Rico become a city island as the environment continues to be neglected?

We've been sold a toxic story in the U.S., and in every corner of the world, that to exist is to consume. In the hierarchy of wealth, with alpha countries ruling the message and developing nations being submissive to the dominant forces, the story is ever-present and heavy-handed. Not only do we need to consume, but the more we consume, and the faster we consume, the better off we are.

Perhaps this means that the stress on la isla madre will handicap El Yunque's ability to protect her from what is lurking in the underworld. And that one day, as she trembles awaiting him, he will not be able to return to her. Fury will rise up out of the sea, and Borikén will become violent with her shaking, caused by the terror of awaiting her beloved. What will happen then?

I never met my mother's father, who passed on when I was nine. I met my mother's mother, once, after she had had a stroke. She was wide and doughy, her flesh overflowing the sides of her wheelchair. In a Catholic nursing home somewhere in the Twin Cities, a month and a half after my eighteenth birthday, I fed this stranger, my grandmother, instant coffee thickened into a hot paste with cornstarch. She gummed the white plastic spoon after I blew on it. Close to eighty, she was paralyzed on her right side. Her tongue, a broken wing. She could not speak. She could not say, "Mucho gusto nieta, mi amor." When I walked into her room, first, my mother trailing behind me, she began to howl. I was the age my mother was when they had last seen each other. The sound was so mournful I nearly blacked out. The agony, or was it relief, was indescribable. The following year, she died.

Silver cup, ceramic ladle, coconut husk bowl. Vessels to hold what is too weak to hold shape on its own. A basket of orchids, basket of vines, basket of ribs. Interlaced, interwoven, knitted together.

When my grandmother was pregnant with my mother, I was there, one of the eggs in my mother's blossoming ovaries. In this way, each pregnant woman, when carrying a girl, carries within her generations.

I imagine a woman who exists beyond time, full of seeds. All the women who have contributed to the composition of my existence are there, in her womb. I long to see their faces, know their names, hear them call to me. I have to make it up, as if it were a fairy tale. I have to imagine who we've been in order to fully be who I am.

It seems as if Puerto Rico has been in a state of perpetual drowning. Along with climate change and the rising waters are other kinds of rising waters. The financial catastrophe, debts to the mainland unable to be repaid—and with none of the U.S. businesses' taxes going to the island, how could it? Hurricanes, more destructive than ever before, the lives lost, the power grids and utilities failing. Earthquakes crumbling buildings, while predatory investors buy up neighborhoods, make public beaches inaccessible, expand the divide between the wealthy gated sections of the island and what have been referred to as "ghettos"—the people within them needing to be swept away.

In the first six months of 2022, six of the island's seventy-eight mayors were charged with public corruption—accepting money in exchange for government contracts—and arrested by the FBI. The resignation of Governor Ricardo Rosselló in 2019 was fueled by grassroots efforts, with Colectiva Feminista en Construcción (Women's Collective Under Construction) leading the charge. The colectiva was founded in 2017 and is inclusive of all women who want to join the fight for women's rights, including LGBTQIA2S+ rights. Mass street protests called for Rosselló to step down ("Renuncia, Ricky!"), and in demonstrations in front of his house in San Juan, Plena Combativa—the sharp edge of traditional music to wield justice—was played. All led to positive change, the hiring of representatives to implement policies that reflect, serve, and protect the people.

Meanwhile, groups like the United Confederation of Taíno People, participating in the International Indigenous Peoples Movement, as they have for the last thirty years, called for immediate attention to the destruction of wetlands and sacred sites. On the podcast *Native America Calling*, Tai Pelli, a prominent voice within the community, demanded protection for Puerto Rico, which has "the largest amount of archeological sites per square [mile]" anywhere in the United States.

In 2012, the United Confederation of Taíno People became my community as well, although I observe it from a distance. Rather than behave as a fully functioning member, I join the festivities on rare occasions. During the pandemic, my involvement increased as I attended online events where I could learn and be reminded through their voices of my heritage, what coherence calls itself, how it speaks, how it names in its own language.

Pelli continues by describing the island government as "a puppet of what the empire does," one that does not allow the gente, Boricuas, to exercise "free, prior, and informed consent" as it relates to the treatment of public lands, a right. Among these battles, Pelli outlines, is also the fight for Taínos to be included as a federally recognized tribe—both by the Puerto Rican government and the U.S. government. "An island that is not self-governing, that continues to undergo colonization and gentrification, continues to be silenced. Behind the façade propped up for the tourists are voices demanding to be heard."

Before I "returned" for the first time, in my early thirties, Puerto Rico shimmered in my imagination, the distant mother island. A place that held the answers my own mother did not have. I was not immune to fetishizing it in a way not altogether different from how a tourist would. This illusion, this ignorance of distance, transmuted as I became obsessed with finding within my own family dynamics the same kinds of drowning that were happening on the island. Within my family was a replica of Puerto Rico's history and politics, including mainland-island relations. But when turning to both my family and to the island, I try to see beyond the pain of being in a perpetual state of "neglect, abandonment, invisibility, identity theft, imposed religion, and environmental racism," as Tai Pelli expressed. Instead, I reach for the qualities inherent in our origins—strength and beauty, resourcefulness and joy, a flourishing beyond mere survival.

Tatarabuela, how old were you when the stroke bent and stapled you to the chair? Do you know what my mami says about you? That you were darker than a raisin, your head covered in braids. How did you talk after your mouth broke? All nine of your nietos on their knees, praying at your feet as if you were Christ himself.

Lift up thy eyes.

Lift up thy hearts.

What was the last thing you needed to tell them while they waited for you to get up? They believed you would rise, fixed as before, and make tostones for them to eat, bathe them in the yard, kiss each of their different-colored faces, loving them all just the same. One sibling held hands with another, who held hands with my mami—hands holding hands and more hands holding until you, Tatarabuela, were in the middle of a circle. They surrounded the island of you and *prayed, if that is what you call the act of begging God. In that moment in our family's history, a rare force of cohesion.*

How different life would be if there had been a miracle and you had been healed. How different if they had known just how broken the thing they loved most could be.

Negra: Negress. Negrota: Young negress. Palida: Pale. Paraíba: From Paraíba. Parda: Brown. Parda-clara: Light brown. Parda-morena: Brown morena. Parda-preta: Black-brown. Polaca: Polish woman. Pouco-clara: Not very light. Pouco-morena: Not very dark-complexioned. Pretinha: Black—either young, or small. Puxa-para-branco: Somewhat toward white. Quase-negra: Almost negro. Queimada: Sunburnt. Queimada-de-praia: Beach sunburnt. Queimada-de-sol: Sunburnt.

There are the ways others see us. Take your pick from among the Puerto Ricans in American media—singers, dancers, actors, performers. Another version of *West Side Story*, as if that were what is needed.

What kind of Puerto Rican are you?

The comments from those who've visited the island could be summed up like this:

Oh, Puerto Rico. I've been there . . .

It-was-so-dirty-so-beautiful-you-are-so-dirty-so-beautiful-the-music-the-dancing-the-rum-the-passion-it-was-so-exotic-you-are-so-exotic-I-could-live-there-I-could-buy-there-I-could-buy-you-let-me-have-it-let-me-have-you-I-own-it-you.

Then there are the "hinchos," the "Yankees," speaking to me in Spanish, surprised when I can't entirely understand them. All that is unspoken between us as to why this is. The heat and pulse of that pain. The pause, waiting for me to perform Boricua for them.

The Nuyoricans they have known. More than I have. In my lifetime thus far, I have been to the island more times than I've been to New York City.

There is an unconscious intimidation in these exchanges, among other feelings that swamp me. To know my culture, my language(s), my island history and to demonstrate these, behave them, is a way of being I've yearned for.

On the island, I possess the ability to blend, except when I open my mouth. Then, I give myself away. I take too long to go "home." My visits mostly happen in my thirties, when I have the time and money to travel, as well as the invitations and connections that make my trips possible. In my forties, there is work, there is just making ends meet, there is my own child to prioritize.

My loyalty and devotion seem akin to what Juan Antonio Corretjer expresses in his poem "Boricua en la Luna." Despite not being born and raised on the island as my mother was, as an island orphan, I claim what she was forced to discard, what she was unable to claim herself. As if that will give me a wholeness, and through that wholeness a barrier of protection she could never provide.

I want to blame her for the rupture, for the trauma of generational disconnect.

I continue to blame her.

Even though she, too, has been torn away from herself, again and again, her entire life. A mechanism that has been grinding for centuries, impacting us both.

When "Pa'lante" is cried, in a unifying call for Boricuas to rally and survive, it's only the echo I hear, so many thousands of miles away from the island's shores.

"Boricua" is a name I learned to call myself. The idea was never suggested by my mother. That would have gone against her instruction for me to blend and avoid attention, an attempt to shield me from the daily threat of being extinguished by any random stranger well-versed in the practice of their own privilege. All the aggressions, micro and macro. We were infected by the message: To be who you are will bring you harm. Protecting yourself from others meant protecting yourself from yourself. But these decisions left us empty, like wrappers littering the mainland. What we needed was access to our deep, intact root systems and structures.

As a young person, I mostly believed my mother, that we were almost white, or something that existed between white and some other unspoken color. If we were not white, if we were not like all those whom we surrounded ourselves with in those small rural Ohio towns, then how could we function? The self-delusion was at our own expense. I suffered the fool for my formative years. Clearly others could see the truth and treated me accordingly. But I was afraid, distrusting what was so obvious.

When I started calling myself Boricua, in my thirties, I began to acknowledge my mother's people, my people, my grandfather and my grandmother, their grandparents, and so on. I acknowledged that before the invaders, the colonizers, came my people, the Taíno, who were thriving on the island, and that braided into their presence, in my own DNA, is also the presence of the stolen and the enslaved, my relatives from West Africa, as well as those who arrived from Europe, primarily Spain, thinking falsely that they had discovered a new world. Perhaps because of the reality of my own family's composition, for me in the label "Boricua" is the inherent understanding of being mixed. We have been mixed and mixing for over five hundred years and counting. It's how we survived.

———

I remember visiting the island in 2010 and feeling my grandmother's presence as I watched, as if standing apart.

Stuffed between shops, restaurants, Dominican vendors in the streets, crowds of people—viejos, families, babies on hips, niños in strollers—stands Plaza del Mercado. A one-story Puerto Rican wonder of chaos. In the streets outside its doors, lines of stubborn shoppers block cars as they try to pass. Window displays feature mannequins in small tight minidresses stretched across their full breasts and bowling balls for nalgas, glittering high-heeled sandals on their feet. Payless, Bakers, Wildflower, Subway, and perfumerías all beckon affordability. Sally's Beauty Supply reigns.

Women and their hair—bleached hair, gray hair, black hair, copper hair, almost always curly hair slicked into ponytails or tied into braids or buns or wrapped around their heads, curls springing defiant from tight holds onto brown necks, perhaps a sign of inherited, biological resistance. Or, less manicured, hair held in place with long flat clips. Women taking care of their business out in the world while their hair does its thing. Sometimes they put a bandana over it. Sometimes, most often, not. I have pictures of my mother, pregnant with me, her hair in the same configuration of clips and pins, hidden beneath a bandana. These women are everywhere. These women are busy holding up the world.

There's no AC in Plaza del Mercado. It's steamy, and the floors are gray with dirt or from being worn thin, I can't tell. The lighting is dim. It enters from the giant windows in the front, but toward the back, where the windows get smaller and higher, it gets darker. Overhead, fluorescent lights take over the job, but poorly. Two herbal booths with natural tinctures, supplements, crammed to the ceiling with small shelves crowded with bottles in Spanish, English, Chinese. Produce vendors all selling the same thing: roots with hairy bark, extra-large avocados, and mangos the size of footballs. Papaya, bananas, plantains, tomatoes, eggplants that are lavender—barely—instead of royal purple and longer than they are wide, ginger, beans. A butcher with red cuts of meat that look swollen and still bleed. Seafood as gray as the floor and dull under glass resting on ice. Pork quarters hanging from above the man selling pig, the fat covering the meat pearly yellow and dense.

An older woman, past sixty-five, whose life I imagine has worn her down, walks into the mercado as I walk out. She wears a T-shirt that says SEXY in cursive glitter, her breasts inching toward her navel even though there is evidence of a bra. I see its straps underneath the white transparent T-shirt. A skirt, just above her knees, pink and red, like the butcher's meat, thick trunks of legs, stalks from the thigh to the ankle, covered in varicose veins that puff and pulse like blue earthworms just beneath the surface, cellulite and loose skin continuously shimmying with every step she takes. She shuffles one foot then the other in pink flip-flops with small bows decorating the wedge that fits between her toes. Her long gray hair with its coils of curls is slicked back. I spot the one strand that escaped.

A dark-skinned girl, perhaps eight or nine years old, dances salsa absentmindedly as she waits for her mother to pay for her dress. Two young girls in a booth selling T-shirts and coffee mugs that spell BORIN-QUÉN dance with each other behind the counter. It's nothing special, a body gesturing, hips pulsing, natural, but dancing is nothing here. Clearly. It's like chewing food, like blinking.

I am fascinated by the women's bodies, as I am by the trees, the flowers, the shrubs. Women wearing strips of dresses, their round breasts peeking through, their round thighs mounds underneath. Their perfume throws me off, and I have to close my eyes to fight off a dizzy spell. My back against a tree, I feel safer with its support of bark, its unseen net of roots. Women's bodies—those of my mami, my tías, my abuela—are mine, are not mine, as I am and I am not these women, this tree, these flowers, these shrubs. Women wearing dresses that reveal everything I want and try to hide at the same time. Modest? Embarrassed? The way the women decorate themselves—with heels and jewelry bought on the cheap at the Plaza Mercado de Diego. If I commit to wearing this costume, will I become more like them? Exposed. Assured.

A woman walks down Avenida Juan Ponce de León holding hands with her boyfriend and her sister, who is close to her age. Late teens, early twenties? Reminds me of being in bed with my ma—her in the middle, a man on the other side, his hand holding on, too. And us wishing it would last.

On my way to and from the market, I pass under a giant mother tree. It makes me happy to see her beauty, ripe and raw. The trees here stop me in my tracks. I feel them, their roots, their extensions, and the expanse of green canopies. Looking up toward the heavens, I am in awe of them—magnificent masterpieces of growth and extension, twists and suspensions in an ancient geological dance. Plants I've tried to grow in the house climb up the trees, tumble off branches, lift in midair, and turn toward the sun.

Under a tree outside the train station, I step around a fist of fruit in shades of green and blush. It takes me a moment, then I realize what it is. I haven't been able to identify any fruit until now. Only the smell of overripe syrup, rotting fragments of flesh and seed and pulp, the heat and humidity turning it into a sweet stench. This time, I know what it is—a jewel, a mango—and it takes me back to the story my mother used to tell, about the sound of mangos falling to the ground at dawn.

All day I feel the spirit of abuela negra. She follows me, holds my hand, whispers, encourages me, soothes me. I wonder how far back she goes. It feels like my mother's grandmother, her face in my own grandfather's face, in my mother's face, in mine. I ache for my heart to be held. It hurts. There is so much beyond words that I will never know how to capture, how to communicate, release.

Regular: Regular, normal. Retinta: Deep-dyed, very dark. Rosa: Rose-colored (or the rose itself). Rosada: Rosy. Rosa-queimada: Sunburnt-rosy. Roxa: Purple. Ruiva: Redhead. Russo: Russian. Sapecada: Singed. Sarará: Yellow-haired negro. Sarauba (poss. dialect): Untranslatable. Tostada: Toasted. Trigo: Wheat. Trigueira: Brunette. Turva: Murky. Verde: Green. Vermelha: Red.

On my birth certificate, it says the mother, mine, is Hispanic, Caucasian. It is a lie. I've met our family. I've seen photos of my grandfather, met my cousins still living on the island. My mother referred to others in her family as Black but never herself. We weren't to refer to ourselves as such. This contradiction created a kind of internal chaos that was crazy making.

Until recently, race in Puerto Rico has been seen as secondary to nationality—Puerto Rican—and ethnicity, "Hispanic" or "Latinx." I wonder if this has something to do with those historically in power and their control over the Puerto Rican narrative at large being primarily light-skinned folks and white-passing Puerto Ricans taking their cues from the U.S. while those with darker skin, those closer to their/our African ancestry and their/our Indigenous ancestry have had their voices, perspectives, and experiences muffled, sidelined.

While color is held differently in Caribbean families, as our sisters, brothers, parents, grandparents, aunts, uncles, and cousins often vary from very dark to very light and all skin tones in between, it does not mean color does not matter. While all are included and (hopefully) loved, there is still the messaging that lighter is better, and there is the distinction of pelo malo and pelo bueno. Clearly, there is a preference. Colorism is active and applied even within families.

My mother's behavior was not something she invented or even learned in the U.S., though she did perfect it here, and her views contained a particular narrowness influenced by American racism. Rather, it was something her own family and the social structures of the island communicated to her as a young child before her time in the mission. When her own Afro-Taíno father told her not to marry a man who was darker than him, it was as if he were holding the line's edge of what was acceptable, and just beyond him lay what was intolerable.

It was not just my mother; other Puerto Ricans throughout this time—the 1970s—and well into the 1980s, 1990s, and early 2000s claimed to be "white" despite it not being true. Being from a colony/territory of the U.S. does not make you white, nor does a white husband make you white. The blanket term "Hispanic" does not make you white. Being "Puerto Rican" does not keep you from being something other than white.

I put my focus into trying to verbalize what was in some ways a family secret. The secret of her, of our origins. It was as if we had an agreement that if I truly loved my mother, I would not fully see her, would not give her away. I didn't so much see her growing up as I smelled her and felt her and heard her. If I truly saw her, I'd betray her. If I saw myself, and her, and others saw me correctly—as a woman of mixed heritage, which included being of African descent—such a moment would not be an opportunity to feel recognized, or a moment to behold, but instead a moment to fear, to dread, and therefore a moment to avoid.

My mother was never able to say, *I am a Black Puerto Rican woman, albeit light-skinned. I am an Indigenous Puerto Rican woman, Taíno, even though I do not know the language, the stories, or the prayers. In addition to the Spanish ancestry, the lineage of whiteness I've championed, there is more.*

With my two older sisters, my mother didn't have to say anything. Their identities went undetected. But her third and final daughter came out looking like her, except for eye color and curl texture. She did not adjust herself or her mothering with the love, attention, and modeling I needed. Instead, she continued in her pattern that served the dominant culture's needs over her child's needs. Her behavior denied her and me our rightful experience of fully existing and expressing, even if only in our home. A learned blindness.

In the practice of seeing myself, I have to confront the blindness, that learned behavior. Acknowledge what drove and perpetuated the devotion to racial/identity ambiguity. I wish it was as simple as looking in the mirror and seeing myself.

Do I see a woman of Puerto Rican descent with ancestors who are Black, brown, and white? A mixed-race woman? A woman of color?

Yes.

Always.

But when I pull apart the sections and try to make them stand on their own, it becomes harder to see myself.

Do I see a Black woman, albeit lighter-skinned?

Yes.

Sometimes.

Do I see a Native woman, brown-skinned?

Yes.

Sometimes.

Do I see a mixed-race woman who shows signs of her father's Irish ancestry?

Yes.

Rarely.

I wonder if it is something to do with the word *see*. To see, to be seen, depends entirely on the eyes, and even if they contain perfect vision, they are still limited and unreliable. As Anaïs Nin said, "We don't see things as they are, we see them as we are." There is an inherent problem in clearly seeing one another, and in clearly seeing ourselves. *See* has become a word that, when applied to my own experience, can trigger my identity trauma. When caught in the crosshairs of a seeing that cannot contain all of me, I dissociate. My vision blurs, I have trouble remembering and articulating myself, I suddenly shrink into a version of myself that is six, or nine, or thirteen, or seventeen, or twenty-five. A heaviness descends, a lethargy that pulls me to bed, where I turtle in, safe from the world and all its eyes. Until my mid-thirties, this fragmentation and contortion, a result of the violence of being made to explain and to prove, dictated much of my life.

Years later, I'm still in a kind of recovery. It's rare that this dissociation happens now, at forty-five, but in unearthing these memories and stories and trying to accurately articulate them, I have reactivated my identity trauma. I hold the word *see* and turn it over and over and over in my hand. It's been a relationship of failure on all accounts. I need another word altogether.

I consider Ralph Ellison's *Invisible Man* and the ways that book spoke to the systematic erasure of the Black man, and of the Black experience in the United States. I consider other Black authors who have come to be known as American historical figures, who have spoken to the complexity of being Black in America—Toni Morrison, Alice Walker, and Dr. Maya Angelou, among others. In all my considering, I land on a quote from James Baldwin: "Justice is an act of witnessing."

In January 2022, Mustafa Ahmed, the Canadian poet turned singer-songwriter, in an interview on *Clique X,* spoke about justice, the act of justice, as being seen. "Justice is when a person is able to carry the many identities and multitudes that a person carries. When they're able to carry that in a way that doesn't feel like any of those identities are compromised or any of those identities are made invisible by another person," he said. "That when someone looks at me, none of those identities are made invisible. None of those identities are compromised, not by systems of oppression, not by educational systems, not by other people, not by living standards, and not by gentrification processes."

These Black authors, creatives, thinkers, social commentators speak to being seen as integral to being considered fully human. The primary relationship with the act of seeing is how they see themselves. The secondary relationship with the act of seeing is how they see others. The tertiary relationship with the act of seeing is how they are seen. There is the promise of clarity and confidence in this order. It is set up for self-possession even in the face of domination—systematic, institutionalized, often violent forces of the overculture's habituation toward white body supremacy as it is articulated through our social and political structures, through patriarchy, imperialism/ongoing colonization, racism, and capitalism.

———

I wish it were as simple as seeing myself with my own eyes, but there are many lenses, and they change. Which lens am I looking through? The Caribbean lens? The Puerto Rican lens? The Spanish lens? The Afro lens? The Taíno lens? The U.S. white lens? The U.S. Black lens? The U.S. Native lens? The BIPOC lens at large? The mixed-race lens? And what about the angle, and the light, and the time of day, and the time of year, and the focus—what part of myself am I looking at, exactly? Because I've been conditioned to be a thing of parts. Not wholly this or that but parceled.

My training tells me that my own lens should depend on that of those around me. That I cannot accurately see myself on my own. Coming of age in Ohio, there were moments I tried to assert my own perception of myself, but then I waited for it to be affirmed by others, waited to be told whether I was correct or incorrect. At seventeen, I remember filling out college applications. I checked multiple boxes: "Hispanic," "Black, African American," and "Native American." The admissions office at one of the colleges I'd applied to called and asked for clarity. Only one box could be checked. My eldest sister, considering her own appearance and identity and reception in the world, nothing at all like my own, checked the "Hispanic" box. It was 1994. Thirty years later, there are many times I still feel as though I'm made to choose one part of my identity over another. That not all can be simultaneously included. That all the parts of me I try to make a cohesive whole are separated again by the limitations of the seer and the projections they make, which for so long I've used to undermine my own experience of myself.

It has been a constant labor. Seeing.

Seeing myself is a complicated task given my composition, given not living on the island, given being raised in Ohio—an intolerant place that championed whiteness. Seeing myself is more something I do through sensing, through feeling. It feels like I am crossing a river. My left foot on a stone, my right foot on another stone. Temporary footing. For a moment, I can see myself. The water is wide and deep and rushing. All that force, all those external forces, those lenses. I'm trying to cross to the other side, where there is solid ground, certainty. I am fighting not to be washed away and lose myself entirely as I have so many times before. This is not Oshún's river water, a liminal space, divine crossroads. Or is it? I am forced to grow my strength, to learn how to keep my balance. My identity is still evolving. I am unfinished. I don't know what I'll say or know tomorrow. What I'll be able to see.

The word *see* has failed me. It is rife with trouble, with harm. Instead,

I choose the word *recognize,* as in to have known before and to know again, as in to acknowledge the existence of, according to the definition in the *Oxford English Dictionary.* I recognize myself by way of all my senses, by an external and internal experience, by the presence of the seen and the unseen, a community that reflects me back to myself, and by my ancestors.

In 2021, as I promote my first book, giving readings and meeting with readers online, I recognize myself in other women writers of color, in Black and Native women writers, in Latinx communities of readers and writers. I recognize myself in the Brooklyn Caribbean Literary Festival as a presenter on a panel and in the pre-event meetings with the wider community of presenters and organizers. In 2022, I recognize myself as I interview two women writers of the Caribbean diaspora whom I cherish, admire, and am continuously inspired by, Myriam Chancy and Tiphanie Yanique. As I allow the parts of myself that have been exiled, those in my family line who have been categorically and systematically sent away—over years, decades—to return to me, calling and singing and dancing all fragments of myself home to me, my recognition shifts, grows. Recognition, in fact, feels like it is an ongoing presence of increasing awareness. I can hold on to that; I can even surrender to it.

I am part of a larger movement of reclamation and celebration, of protest and demands for change, among Boricuas. Out of resilience and resistance is surging a gathering of all that had to be subdued, shed, and stored away. Many are claiming and including what they are, naming their racial components. Black. Native. I am doing the same. We are finally understanding more fully the existence of our ancestors. They are not dead and gone. They are very much alive and well, articulating themselves through and with us.

In an interview with Georges Collinet on the radio show *Afropop Worldwide,* Puerto Rican music folklorist Nelie Lebron-Robles alludes to this when discussing Black identity among Puerto Ricans. When speaking about the evolution of bomba and plena, traditional island music rooted in the place and people of Loíza, Lebron-Robles says that the music has become a symbol of Black pride. "Over time, from the end of the '90s until now, bomba has transformed from something negative, an ignorant part of society, into something to be proud of, part of our national identity. Up to that time, national identity was basically composed of our Spanish/Latin American and Taíno cultural heritage. That third [African] part of our identity as a people was not looked upon as something that you should be proud of," Lebron-Robles explains. "But it's this other part of our identity that is important. They used to call it '*la tercera raíz*,' the third root, and I think from then on, Puerto Rico started to understand that we cannot be who we are if we don't recognize and acknowledge our Blackness, our negritude, and so it has started to transform something, especially in the younger generation, to be something [to be] very proud of . . . Black, without it being insulting."

I am now privileging those who have been systematically silenced and erased within my heritage. It is a practice I engage in my bio, and every time I have a public speaking event, or teach a new group of students, or give a reading, or am interviewed, or interview others, no matter, I introduce myself—I am a Boricua woman. I am Afro-Taína. I am not the daughter of a white woman. I am the daughter of a Black Puerto Rican woman, a Black and Indigenous/Taína Puerto Rican woman, who hid behind her ethnicity and nationality of being Hispanic, of being Puerto Rican, because of the reinforcement both on the island and on the mainland that lighter was better.

I acknowledge the ancestral homelands where I am standing, and I also acknowledge the peoples within me, as all of these are in relationship—the territory in which I stand, and my ancestors because of whom I can stand, at any given moment. I do this in Spanish, and I do this in Taíno, not because I'm fluent in either language, not as a performance, but because it's part of my ongoing practice of rematriating my identity. My practice of seeing, naming, including, and claiming my identity works against the constant force of erasure, an eroding riverbank I must shore up with my whole being, with my entire presence.

This is my name; this is who lives within me and who has been silenced. I will no longer contribute to the silence or the secrecy of their existence.

I reach toward the island—toward the east, where new birth, hope, and possibilities are imbued—and I reach for something more substantial.

Sovereignty.

There is nation sovereignty, which federally recognized tribal nations in the U.S. have. More than what Puerto Rico has. There are the policies put into place by sovereign nations, the respect for how they vision, govern, and rule.

But as a descendant of Afro-Taíno peoples, as a person, a woman, from the Caribbean diaspora, a Boricua, I am reaching for a sovereignty that exists elsewhere. That sits in the courage center of the heart, in the truth and connection with the authority of selfhood. Beyond the generational traumas and victimizations, I am reaching for sovereignty in my creativity, my imagination, beyond the limits of anyone or anything, where envisaging is limitless.

For now, I have come to visualize myself as a chichigua. High in the air above El Morro, I fly beyond la isla madre, yet I am attached by a delicate but secure string, an umbilical cord, a heart line, the mother root. Securely tethered to ancestral hands that do not necessarily provide the answers I am looking for but instead provide a connection with what transcends words.

"I told a story until it transformed . . .
I could feel the grace notes."

—STORME WEBBER, *GRACE NOTES*

CHANGING SHAPE,
PART II

WIND WHIPS THROUGH THE OPEN WINDOWS OF MY mother's Buick. An early-morning summer haze lifts from Ohio fields interrupted by squat cement buildings, a mix of agricultural and industrial landmarks. The tar-filled cracks on the two-lane highway vibrate through the wheels—*ba-bump, ba-bump, ba-bump*—a rhythm that puts me to sleep only to jolt me awake. The traffic lights are few and far between. I can smell my mother's perfume, see the ends of her hair twirling in a dance with the wind. Lying on the back seat, I watch the side of her face, revealed when her hair lifts.

I'm asleep. I'm awake. I'm asleep.

I'm awake again, and when I sit up, the car is still driving at speed, moving forward, the wheel slightly adjusting now and then to keep between the lines. But my mother is not in the driver's seat. My mother is not in the car. I'm alone. I look through the windshield as the car continues to be driven past the fields, past the occasional bunker of a building.

I do not remember this as a dream. I remember it as truth. This was my reality.

———

My mother gave birth three times. Three wishes. Three little girls. Three attempts to see herself, treat herself the way she wished she'd been treated.

The task proved to be too much. Instead of focusing on us, she kept her focus tightly directed on herself. Her life force held in a riptide of wounding.

I can't imagine what she thought or felt as she collapsed for the afternoon—the evening, the weekend, the month, the year—with us pulling at her and demanding attention she did not have to give. Beneath her response to us, which was typically full of tired words, incoherent excuses, or nonsensical stories, was all that went unnamed swimming in the dark waters beneath.

It seemed instead that she used us as three chances to turn us into the mother she never had. I, her last try, suffered her the worst. My refusal to mother her the strongest.

———

In my third trimester, I reconnected with a therapist, a curandera of sorts, who had never failed to provide clarity when my life situations had grown toxic—another boyfriend with narcissistic tendencies I couldn't seem to quit, a PhD program that threatened my health, a housing agreement gone terribly wrong, my mother's constant false and/or emotional emergencies. In the past, my therapist would name the situation, directly and succinctly, ask if I agreed, and then invite me to act with the new awareness gained from the session. She taught me to choose in the interest of my own well-being. I had learned to mother myself, and soon, I would learn how to mother my own child.

With my delivery date approaching, I wanted insight and comfort.